The BreakBeat Poets Series

ABOUT THE BREAKBEAT POETS SERIES

The BreakBeat Poets series is committed to work that brings the aesthetic of hip-hop practice to the page. These books are a cipher for the fresh, with an eye always to the next. We strive to center and showcase some of the most exciting voices in literature, art, and culture.

The BreakBeat Poets Advisory Board:
Kevin Coval (series editor), Nate Marshall, Idris Goodwin, José Olivarez, Safia Elhillo, Maya Marshall & Mahogany Browne

BREAKBEAT POETS SERIES TITLES INCLUDE:

The BreakBeat Poets: New American Poetry in the Age of Hip-Hop,
    edited by Kevin Coval, Quraysh Ali Lansana, and Nate Marshall

This Is Modern Art: A Play, Idris Goodwin and Kevin Coval

The BreakBeat Poets Vol 2: Black Girl Magic,
    edited by Mahogany L. Browne, Jamila Woods, and Idrissa Simmonds

Human Highlight, Idris Goodwin and Kevin Coval

On My Way to Liberation, H. Melt

Black Queer Hoe, Britteney Black Rose Kapri

Citizen Illegal, José Olivarez

Graphite, Patricia Frazier

The BreakBeat Poets Vol 3: Halal If You Hear Me,
    edited by Fatimah Asghar and Safia Elhillo

Commando, E'mon Lauren

Build Yourself a Boat, Camonghne Felix

Milwaukee Avenue, Kevin Coval

Bloodstone Cowboy, Kara Jackson

Everything Must Go, Kevin Coval, illustrated by Langston Allston

Can I Kick It?, Idris Goodwin

Too Much Midnight, Krista Franklin

The BreakBeat Poets
Volume 4

Edited by
Felicia Rose Chavez
José Olivarez
and
Willie Perdomo

Haymarket Books
Chicago, Illinois

© 2020 Felicia Rose Chavez, José Olivarez, and Willie Perdomo

Published in 2020 by
Haymarket Books
P.O. Box 180165
Chicago, IL 60618
773-583-7884
www.haymarketbooks.org
info@haymarketbooks.org

ISBN: 978-1-64259-219-1

Distributed to the trade in the US through Consortium Book Sales and Distribution (www.cbsd.com) and internationally through Ingram Publisher Services International (www.ingramcontent.com).

This book was published with the generous support of Lannan Foundation and Wallace Action Fund.

Special discounts are available for bulk purchases by organizations and institutions. Please email orders@haymarketbooks.org for more information.

Cover artwork by Yvette Mayorga.
Cover design by Brett Neiman.

Printed in the United States.

Library of Congress Cataloging-in-Publication data is available.

Contents

Willie Perdomo

Breakbeat, Remezcla

In March 2004, I was invited to Santiago, Chile to celebrate Pablo Neruda's centennial. If you've been to Chile, you know that it's a poet's country. Copies of novels by Isabel Allende and poetry by Nicanor Parra are sold in subway vending machines like so many cans of sugary drinks or bags of potato chips. Taxi drivers and hotel clerks are well-versed in Neruda. If you walk through any market, you can hear the chant, "Libros! Libros, baratos." In Chile, it's not uncommon to look up and find that poems are being dropped from helicopters like bombs.

Along with workshops and visits to schools, there were the mandatory readings and performances. On a crisp Friday night, I was the featured poet in an event at Plaza Camilo Mori, which is located in the center of Barrio Bellavista. The stage was a portable lift on which I was raised to overlook the plaza. I read an ode to Chile, poetry, and Neruda that I had written the night before and that was generous in its use of Spanglish. At the end of my reading, the plaza erupted into an applause and affirmation that one might find at a political rally. My use of English and Spanish was a revelation to some of the poets in the crowd. The audience in Plaza Camilo Mori had never heard Spanish and English in a poem. They were witnessing a *LatiNEXT* moment. For some of them, it was something new. For me, I was like: *This is what we do.*

The BreakBeat Poetry Series offers a poetics that, like hip-hop, is in constant search of new forms, new utterances, new languages, freshness. Every day a new regulation, a new assault, is hoisted on the Black and Brown bodies of this country whether they are immigrants or native sons. If poetry is truly a decolonial practice, then this anthology lifts its lyrical machete, its formalistic authority, its innovative approach toward language, its queerness, its nonbinary *they*, its sense of lineage, family, tradition, pride, and, refreshingly, its Blackness. You will find poems by Elizabeth Acevedo, Raquel Salas Rivera, Sara Borjas, John Murillo, Daniel Borzutsky, and Vincent Toro—poets who are in conversation, in celebration, in protest, in demonstration, in a collective breakbeat that is informed by ritual, but also a resistance to the normalized ways of looking at stanzas, patria, sex, gender, patriarchy, and nationalism. This anthology is standing right next to the street activists and professors, slam poets and National Book Award winners, MCs, and youth poets. And it does so humbly, aggressively, fearlessly, jokingly, multilingually, and, at the right moments, with bravado.

Pablo Neruda, like Amiri Baraka, maintained that if you can't read your poem to a fruit vendor, a construction worker, a crossing guard, then your poem is worthless. The tradition of Latinx poetics ranges from the super elitist traditionalist who still holds on to what Audre Lorde called the "master's tools," to MCs like Big Pun. We rock like that, and we make room at the table for that range. In this book you'll find poets who are at the start of their poet lives, poets who are at the peak of their careers and still trying to challenge themselves, and poets who might not ever write another poem.

The Latinx demographic in the United States has changed. Facts. We are in the majority. Facts. I think the Trumpistas and rabid protectors of the white ethnostate know that we are in a *somos más* moment and that poets might play a key role in that moment. And we should be aware that this is just a sliver of who is out there poeting. We would need another anthology just to accommodate the ever-growing nation of Latinx and Hispanophone Caribbean poets across the nation and abroad.

This past summer, "El Verano de Puerto Rico" combusted when a group of students, rap stars, pop stars, politicians, motorcyclists, scuba divers, poets, grandmothers, activists, and justice warriors, peacefully took to the cobblestoned, colonized streets of San Juan, shouting "Somos más y no tenemos miedo," and demanded the resignation of Ricky Rosselló, a legacy politician who, at the time, was the presiding governor of Puerto Rico. The demand was simple: Ricky had to go. He was exposed as a misogynist who also made fun of residents, mostly poor, who suffered terrible losses in the destructive torrent of Hurricane Maria. At the vanguard of the movement were women with names like "Tita Molotov" who chanted and banged on pots and pans until the governor and his staff listened. Ricky has since resigned, and now the galvanized movement has other targets in its sight: La Junta, disaster capitalists, hedge-fund vultures, and the Jones Act which, to this day, has had an enfeebling effect on Puerto Rico.

Poets, voluntarily or not, consciously or not, are engaged in a moment of resistance to definitions, monolithic stereotypes, and outmoded ways of looking at the Latinx experience. No one has the upper hand or singular authority on being Latinx, queer, trans, biracial, Black, fluent, or claims to the best *pasteles*, *mofongo*, or *horchata*. The *mezcla*, or the *remezcla*, is where we are going to find our strength, our vision, our power, and it's in these pages where you'll find the blueprint, which is simultaneously frightening, magical, and real. Welcome to this *somos más* moment.

Exeter, NH
12 August 2019

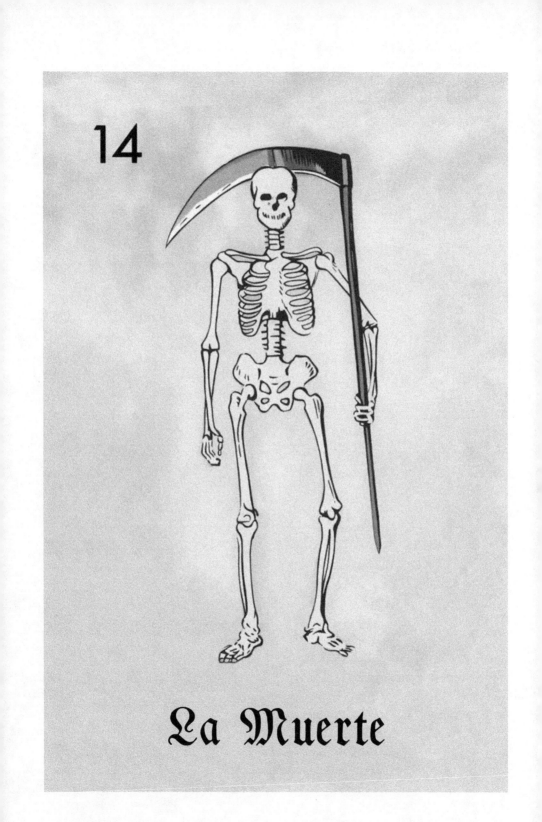

14

La Muerte

Failed Bomba

¡Ecuajey!

We them
>   cane cutters,
>   them peloteros,
>   them goya-bean-eating,
>   always-cooking-
>   with-too-many-spices-
>   *I-don't-wanna-smell-that-shit*

muhfuckas.

Them
>   salsa-and-reggaetón-playing-
>   siempre-hay-una-fiesta-
>   *turn-that-shit-down-already*

muhfuckas.

¿Y qué decimos?
>   *Pa'l carajo.*

We just
>   malcriaos.
We don't know
>   no better.
Can't speak English
>   right,
can't
>   govern ourselves.

Pero we love our bomba
and
>   you keep saying *we*
pero tú no eres real—
>   take out barriles, drum loudest,
>   drown out anyone who calls out
>   your mimicry, self-inflicted bullet wounds

to match Filiberto or maybe Daddy Yankee.
How long you practice
those notes, anglo,
that acento?

Think we won't throw you in the ocean?
Let the tiburones pull you apart?
Just keep playing and you'll see.
¿Ecuajey?

Míja

When my mother calls me míja over the phone,
my vertebra—discordant map of chow
mein and stars, feel saucy. And
even though my lips are rusted,
when mother calls me in Spanish,
the gold loops spiral in me:
the caldo de res
the chopped carrots
the no-measure
cooking the stiff
broom good
for corners
the stubborn
apology
the mangled
love the cacti
exploding
in my molcajete
body—míja,
my first
galaxy my
revolving
door my
stuck door my
smashed window
my pocha leash
my buried
tenderness
what my mother
still wants
her mother
to call
and say

Portrait and Shadow

The curtains sail into the room with the memory of presence behind them

while my father waits in the dark taking apart what is left of his former selves,
  like a pianist, drunk at the keys, playing the same four notes,

letting them ring in the pedals until they haul themselves back into sleep.

He says, *I am shadow*

& the thief at the seam of his spine slides through the blades of his shoulders,
  hollows the blood, while the dopamine cheapens

like a dollar-store lighter & suddenly, another streak in his Depends emerges as
  proof.

This too in Arcadia—

the meadow in twilight's last streak of red before he enters the tree line,

which is already waiting, its small footpaths like paintings held in storage,
  their deep palettes so close they strangle to a labyrinth

laced in an MRI-black. The wolf there tears at his tendons,

leaves him always in fog, & if he emerges it is only to watch but not to enter
  the burning city & self he still loves.

He says, *I am the smoke's mascara*

& I know he is imagining the Bronx he can never return to,
  where his youth is held in the thin frame of a bicycle

as it cuts through a billow of smoke. The city burned each night & each
  morning
  he rose to ride through the rubble. The what was,

8   the father I hold onto in order to care for his shadow never gets old—

he is kind & clear, he rises each morning & lifts me onto the back of his bicycle,
    he pedals while I glide above the city in wonder.

Instructions for My Funeral

Don't burn me in no steel furnace, burn me
    in Abuelita's garden. Wrap me in blue-
white-and-blue [a la mierda patriotismo].
    Douse me in the cheapest gin. Whatever you do,
don't judge my home. Cut my bones
    with a machete till I'm finest dust
[wrap my pito in panties so I dream of pisar].
    Please, no priests, no crosses, no flowers.
Steal a flask and stash me inside. Blast music,
    dress to impress. Please be drunk
[miss work y pisen otra vez].
    Bust out the drums the army strums.
Bust out the guitars guerrilleros strummed
    and listen to the war inside [please
no american mierdas]. Carouse the procession
    dancing to the pier. Moor me
in a motorboat [de veras que sea una lancha]
    driven by the nine-year-old
son of a fisherman. Scud to the center
    of the Estero de Jaltepec. Read
"Como tú," and toss pieces of bread.
    As the motorboat circles,
open the flask, so I'm breathed like a jacaranda,
    like a flor de mayo,
like an alcatraz—then, forget me
    and let me drift.

A Time Magic
for Raffaele

i am writing you a new spell that extends from the spell of your making silver
filament thread that carried your glimmer to lining rest i write you a spell that
in printing will gild the ways possible   in speaking will take shape in your
bone set and salt   your spell will become sung by women who do not know
they are world witches   your spell will be danced in trans spirals of to-know
men will walk in your wake and wonder at your spell manifest i watch you in
this baby form asleep beneath stripes of white and black   you our blend baby
taíno boricua african american italian and so many others who dreamt you from
their heavy feet world marking   your papá and i walk the asphalt path by his
childhood lake   followed by your zii in blood and want i have already begun
to write the spell which exists then and now and in the future will bleed from
your hand cut by a newly opened page i am with you i am not with you i see
you then   a sailor far from water biding the frost time in a mountain keep that
no one loves until you   in your hands an orange-covered book of italian
philosophy from your grandfather's library you read with a sweet smile while
a fire burns   you are firelight cast free i write you the spell of freedom in water
ice   thought grooved on page i write you angelic sheen that you carry on your
cheeks still in this sixth month ever after   the stroller channels gravel in winter's
quiet park time there and as i tap keys my bare feet on white marble while you
sleep in a crib   your papá snores his lullaby   you are there too at a mountain
retreat as your papá was years ago   eighteen and studying for exams a step on
the path toward me and toward you   by my side we saw the place where your
great-grandmother planted two trees   one for him and one for your uncle   one
died only the dead know whose it was   in berkeley there is a fig tree planted
for you   the juice of its first fruit i placed on your infant tongue   time in
you ripples out then back again   water weaving its ephemeral web on current
layers   you are a sign of water born between luck and unluck   free from the
wheels   you make your own making   i give you tales and you are the
teller

Carlos Andrés Gómez

Hijito

for Trayvon Martin and Michael Brown

I am enthralled by the image
in front of me: my face overlaid
with his—a boy, almost a man, inside
the glass of the grocery store
reaching for a branch
of seedless grapes.

This sly mirror. This taut mirage.
A coiling limb slithers in my gut, its roots
(invisible)—like I am on this asphalt
to any soul that is inside, right now,
like he is. Today, she is
nine weeks along, he is almost eighteen,
I am grasping for any thought
that is not my son calling out breathless
from the hollow lungs of night, abandoned
seven feet from the hood of a patrol car
where a hubcap swallows secrets
beside a pavement-choked throat
heaving for breath, his jawline borrowed
from my face, above it a still-shaking
hand crowned by smoke, uniformed
in my skin.

La guitarra llora
When My Parents Meet

Y al ver que inútilmente te envío mis palabras
llorando mi guitarra se deja oír su voz
is what the guitar hustler sings
the day his brown eyes meet her brown eyes,
an off-key song of poverty as passengers swing on and off *el micro*,
the small green busses of Lima.
His jutting headstock swaying with the melody,
serenading eyes that have learned to take no notice.

His brown eyes have learned to take no notice
as vendors shoulder their way through the jungle of limbs,
shouting *tamarindo-chicha-choclo*,
competing with him for spare change.
The arms, legs, and heads crammed in *el micro*
sway as the small green bus swerves around missing manhole covers:
the putrid mist from open sewer lids wrinkles noses.

Amid the overcrowding, the hustlers, the vendors
her brown eyes have learned to take no notice,
so, on this night,
on the way home from the hospital where she is a secretary,
when the sweet garbage stench washes in and
mixes with the body odor of the guitar hustler
shoving a jingling cup into her chest,
she looks over his black hair as the city lights blur past.

Her forehead glistens with humidity; droplets roll down her spine.
Her hair frizzes like blonde cotton candy.
Compressed in the aisle,
her sweaty knuckles brace her to the back of a seat,
and as the guitar hustler moves on, her stare slips,
and her brown eyes meet his brown eyes.

He's seen her get on. He's been waiting to say something,

thinking of the right words as he sings along.
She's the only blonde in a sea of brown,
and in the jungle of legs and sweaty heads and jutting elbows,
his brown eyes meet her brown eyes.
She responds by pushing her way through the people
to exit *el micro*.
There's something about her worth following, so
he shoulders past the tamarindo vendor.
Catches up to her on the street,
grasps for her fingertips, and their eyes meet.

The kiosk sells single cigarettes, and she doesn't even smoke,
but there's something about him worth smoking for.

She coughs, cough-coughs.
Her brown eyes meet his brown eyes, and the
question marks exhaled from her lungs
hang in the air between them
become ellipses,
which he flirts with

Cansado de llamarte, con mi alma destrozada
comprendo que no vienes porque no quiere Dios,
y al ver que inútilmente te envío mis palabras
llorando mi guitarra se deja oír su voz...

What's in a Name?

It is the sound of our identity.
The auditory virtual self
that is spoken into the universe,
and when written on the page
it means "me."

And I was given
Iraida—mi papi me llamo, with tears in his eyes and love blooming in his heart.
Playa playa though he was, I was the sparkle in his winking eye.
And like many ghetto youngins,
he created my name from the name of his wife:
Aida and Iris.
Iraida—mami me llamo, longing and aching for a little girl who would receive
    all the pure, and, she thought,
untainted love that she had to give.
Off to school I went into a world of English-speaking teachers,
with little or no patience for ethnicity.
It was enough that they had to learn all our names, but to say them correctly?
File under: Not Important.
And so the name that Papi proudly crowned me with became:
Eye-ray-duh,
I raid her,
I ate,
I hate her,
Uh-rye-duh,
I ride her.
It sounded like paper tearing.
It was ugly, it was ordinary
it was me.

As I grew
Iraida curled into a ball and sat in my chest,
happily raising her head when she was called.
But otherwise, Jani answered all the questions.
Can you say that right?
"Jani?" they'd ask.

Yeah, like "Jani be good," and since

I have to remind myself, please do not mess with me.
"That's not your real name though, your real name is. . ."
Iraida.
"Well, how do you say that in English?!"
You don't.

How do I explain?
My name, filled with joyful rainbows and eighty-five-degree sun-showers,
became a misshapen abstract loop of auditory nonsense.
Frustration bubbles up as I ask you not to call me Eye-ray-duh
but you'd insist that it's my proper
name and that you will refer to me as such.
That is not my name.
You will not rename me.
I will not shout Toby!
It is MY name!
Historically it has been our pride;
it spoke of our family,
it sang of our culture.

By the time I was nine I wanted a new identity.
I wanted to be Melinda or Linda. Or Barbie.
There were no toothbrushes, key chains, bicycle plates, or T-shirts with my
    name.
That lady on *Romper Room* never ever ever EVER said "Happy birthday" to me.
I determined to change it at eighteen legally,
but needing a quick fix Nina (and then Jani) became my *alter egos*.
I even had a girl in Puerto Rico writing pen-pal letters to a "Brenda."
At eighteen, I would be reborn!
The possibilities were endless!

And then Papi died,
at forty years old he died,
succumbing to poison from another time, another place.
(There's an entirely different poem about militaries and agent orange right here.)
Cancer crept up on us just when I thought I would get to know him,
and by the time it was time
to change my name, I couldn't,
because it was all he had ever given me.
And one day, someone said it right.

16   In my mind,
     in my heart,
     it just sounded right,
     and I fell in love.

     In my name, the coqui chants
     and the flamboyan leans,
     depositing petals onto the veranda,
     sprinkling the ground around Tía's rocking chair
     where it smells of flowers and a cafecito.
     If you say it right,
     turquoise oceans, sparkling in the sun
     like liquid antique glass, bathe your tongue.

     It is mine. Very few have it. It is special.
     And though people see fair skin and eyes,
     there is no doubt that Iraida Janina Perez de Rosado es Boricua.
     If you say it right
     it is a balm to my spirit;
     a gift to my soul.
     Iraidita—Papi me llamó y Mami me cantó
     Y es mi nombre.

Superstition

In Central America,
to whistle in your home meant you were making room for bad luck,
like a man who didn't wipe his feet clean at the door.
It meant you were the inviting host of an evil spirit.
It meant you were asking for your home to be set on fire from the foundation.
In America, people whistle while they work,
whistle while happy,
whistle to call an animal on four legs closer.

Recently I learned how to do this singing with
just my lips, tongue, and breath.
Old habits die hard,
so I only do it outside the house.

I have a fear of meeting the person who will ruin me while whistling,
while happy or attempting to start a fire.
Which means they will be my very own evil spirit on four legs,
the ghost my mother warned me about hissing past the door frame,
the unseen fire starter;
the house will smell like propane and lighter fluid.

While on the train, folks will look around like they just saw a ghost
and ask what smells like it is burning,
and I know they will mean me.
Which translates to me being the one with the dead dog.
Which means they will know I am the one who did not listen to her mother,
who plays with ghosts and doesn't expect
a fire
or man
to burn my house.

Mami Told Me to Put Water under the Bed

When I was seven: hot with fever, small
pocked body searching for relief, my chapped
lips keeping the beat of a body pulsing to an
illness no doctor could find.

When I was fifteen: a vessel for an unsettled
storm and growing resentment, my curves
becoming razor-sharp war stories told
through mouths of boys that had too many teeth.

When I was twenty-three: Abuela's inheritance
of forked uterus and spiked cervix threatened
to scorch my timeline as it had done to hers
too many years too soon.

—*Water would save you*, Mami said—

Water would drown out the death that wanted
so fiercely to map itself onto my back,
pour herself into all the ache, replace
the unknown with ebb and flow, fill me
with a love so hard it could detach me from the fall.

And I came to know water is synonymous
with woman,
with warrior,
with ritual.
My mouth became
a well,
a waterfall,
and finally, a weapon
so sharp, so wet
it could cut the
chaos of any curse.

Water would sever my soul from collapse,
free my head of locks too heavy to hold,
reteach my bones to speak survival,
pour molasses into my seams,
and rise as the ocean claims me as
her daughter over and over again.

Tonight, I will place a glass of cool water
under my bed, listen for the song of my
ancestors that says: *We would never
let you drown.*

Wild Onion
for Shikaakwa

the wild onion is an elephant
it remembers 1492 and 1837
it remembers August, Lucy, and Fred
it will remember Rekia Boyd

the wild onion lives
gun to its head 24/7

its beauty mark, a raised fist

the wild onion is not afraid
calls the skunk place home
insists the rain is not an inconvenience
it helps you grow
thick skin to weather the storm
even when the wind blows and sirens
fill the night wild
seeds always break thru.

Fiao / Rafi

Rafi has a book
black and white
with names:

Rosa
Indio
Virginia
Dulce
Pito

followed by numbers
that gradually increase
as the month goes by.

Rafi's cat stares from bread shelves
as children bring grocery lists
and speak in low voices:

"Rafi, mami dijo if we can have

una libra de ham de sandwich
½ libra de cheese
gallon de milk
y un box of Newports
that she'll pay you el día quince when she gets her food stamps."

Rafi nods
writes down la cuenta
el sabe que la piña está agria—
that times are hard.

He gambles every month
hoping that
Carmen
Michelle
Fido

22 Tata
    y Rodolfo
    pay their debt on time
    and they do.
    Porque la gente know
    Rafi understands.

    That the fifteenth of every month doesn't
    give enough to fill the belly.

    So
    we pay our debt
    Rafi rips the page with numbers
    and we start all over again.

Luanne

Luanne talk in round
Don't know no other shaped language but a circle
Her lip slur, drawl—
It be big mama after she put her foot up on the porch to a whisky swallow
A sinking sway that stays afloat
Luanne mouf the engine on my first car
It rev and stutter and rev and stutter, take forever to get where it's going, but it
    arrives
She eat like she trynna make you jealous
All the food on display and got the nerve to show up with sound to yell it's here
Luanne don't give a fuck
Drool on her ownself outside the house
Smile like nobody ever told her what the TV say beautiful is
Smile like she don't know how she be looking
Like she don't know how to begin to care
Or never caught her own reflection in a storefront window
Like the rest of us wished we hadn't
The boys turn their heads and all the girls laugh in Luanne's face
When she walk out into the school yard
They don't even sideways snicker behind they fingers no mo'
Just laugh a hefty laugh out loud
Act like she hard of hearing too
Luanne in age with the rest of us but still wear bo-bos and twists in ha hair
She wear this faded magenta T-shirt with a cluster of flowers branching from
    the collar

That's her Tuesday/Thursday shirt
Luanne stunts, Luanne repeats
Luanne don't care like us
She authentic, got muscles we all afraid to use
I watch them point and cackle in jealousy
'Cause they don't understand what God did here
She just stay beaming
Stay crooked like the girls call her
Stay special like they taunt
Luanne is special

24   Tantrum on a pretty day
Wreck, quiet, scream a room still
Cackle when something funny
Run when it scares her
Stay when it feel good
Say nothing when she ain't got nothing to say
Don't fake the funk
She don't be polite for nobody's feelings
Tell you she want it, tell you to take it back
Tell you you stupid when you is stupid

One day in the yard
I sit next to her on the grass and we watch the boys run and reach
For the pretty girls
She say the boys round here are just boys and she want a man
Someone with clean hands
I then decide that Luanne will always say the prettiest things
And she just wipe her wet mouth
Laugh again
Like all of this is just her favorite season

Night, for Samuel Cruz
after Aracelis Girmay's "Night, for Henry Dumas"

Samuel Cruz, 1965–2013,
did not die from the pills
of resin needed to still
the spilling paint of his mind,
nor from the man staring
blankly from his canvas,
but was shot in a flash, at forty-eight,
by a New Rochelle police officer,
will be spilt down, May 26th,
in an apartment cluttered with
his thoughts, a wife begging
in the distance, "Can I go to my
husband? Can I talk with him?"
Shot by a New Rochelle police officer,
in his apartment where he changed
his locks like he changed his thoughts
when a brush touched the canvas,
still wet, not just right, not just
right, not just right, until his heart
eases into its thorns and dreams,
happening yesterday, happened tomorrow,
broke, broke, broke, bang(!),
spill down now,
shot down soon,
happening at home & happening in public,
with or without wife,
with or without strangers,
with or without voice,
in New York, California, Pennsylvania,
the Bronx, Washington, Phoenix,
Denver, Texas, 489 Tompkins Avenue,
Rikers Island, Hampton Roads Regional Jail,
above which hangs a blank sheet of flesh
that says paint the portraits of Morales
& Bah

& Rodriguez
     & Zambrano-Montes,
     & Simental
     & Mitchell
     & Anderson
     &
     &
     & the night break through their eyes
     & the nightmares will come to an end,
     I swear, I swear to you every inch of my body
     for your mural, paint every face into blessing.
     Let the violence end with all
     the signatures of your names.

Before the Last Shot

What was I doing at fifteen?
Facedown on the pavement,
nostrils tinged with bullet-smoke,
the brick-dust falling around
us like fresh snow or white
chalk, his lanky silhouette stalking
the abandoned sidewalk.
It was summer, Brooklyn.
Nothing ever happens
until it happens. That's how my brother
and sister-in-law were describing their tours
at war after our dinner in Manhattan.
We had decided to take a shortcut
through Sumner projects, then heard
the unmistakable sound that tore
through the story I was telling about
a lunchtime fight on the blacktop of
my high school, a sudden flash
of lightning: no one believed it
was happening. They forgot their army
training, rubber-necked toward
the source of the thunder. And then we
tumbled behind the parked cars.
Waited. For what, we were not sure.
Between cars, I could only make
out his narrow back and the dark
steel clutched in his small hand.
I needed to see his face, half
expecting to see myself: standing
on the corner aiming at
something that is never quite there.

Notes from the Valley of a Hundred Fires

If I forget you, Israel, let my right hand be severed with *un machetazo*. In the old world a chicken bone fell like rain—they say you can find them even here if you look hard enough. When the man comes we fill our chests with rain. Dirt, too, smells like rain before the reaping. The cartography of loss is condensed milk on a tile floor sticking in the grout and it is entirely too hot here, but when our uncle tried to leave the valley of a hundred fires they put him in the prison *sí, la cárcel*, and if Andy García can't convince you as much then let me tell you what!

There was a road there not too far from Alabama where in the brush were the letters of Paul written in sweet black juice. I plucked the berries from Paul's field thinking *yes, I might die here but at least I will bear the stain of good on my fingers, if only the angel of death would look back from Montgomery and sigh on me before dinner.*

Later I poured dad's whiskey in paper cups on the dirt and cupped the earth in my palms. For a moment it was the earth and not the clouds moving, an island of water like salt eroding borders and moving further from me. I shoved fistfuls of cotton in my mouth so I could be an ageless woman too like the earth rooted in blue water and the wind's reverberation from Galilee to Islamorada to Cienfuegos; so I would have time, you see.

You once said that words were the red clay in August growing upward in wisps when the earth opened its mouth and yawned. You could crack an egg over Jerusalem and it would burn. The mirage was the thing, only it was outside of you, and I walked with the gentiles in their Birkenstocks and where were you?

When the man came we wept into the dust at the rotten fruit all eaten by flies, we all in white before the head of the offering, uncalved, in the burning valley below.

Nahui Ehecatl,
Second Son / Wind Sun: A Revision

> *I am different things on different days.*
> —My tío, Silastino

Under piñon swaying with wind. Thinking of the brother my mother gave away the year I turned six. What is it to lose something—before you knew it was yours to lose? I have not seen my brother in a lifetime. I don't drink. Never had the stomach for it. My eyes close. I am sitting on a porch with my brother. The same breeze on both our faces. Drinking ice-cold Budweisers, laughing, cursing like our tíos did when we were mocosos and nothing more. He has a daughter now. Like our mother she sees through inkwells. Hair as long and ebon as a cormorant's wing. Our mother. Was always his—he was only hers for a short while. Just long enough to teach us one thing:

the greatest act of love (and betrayal)

    any mother can do for (to) her first son

        is to give up her second son

            in a futile attempt

                to save them
                  both.

My eyes open

    and I am brother and nothing more.

Seasonal Without Spring: Summer

I dozed on the handball court in the noon's non-shadow
    until it was hard to see

anything but the splotched sun—

a cut in the reel—

    then the spliced imagination on screen between the actual scenes of my life
    held in a locked room, all through summer.

Was that season artery or vein?

    When the days stretched like Broadway,
    & the nights undid our shirts—

the temperature so slight you could raise your arms in flight & feel nothing,
    the body as air.

But there was also the need for hurt.

And dusk: a ghost of a boy tempted to feel his weight,
    to put his palm to the depth,

touch the pupil, the dead turbine of god's one good cataracted eye.

And the clouds throwing shadows on the reservoir until it was the color
    of Jason's gun—glean & black.

Sweat stains & thirst. The year of my first fight
    & the pavement on my cheek like depression—

Devon at my back screaming, *Get the fuck up.*
    Blood on a leaf, one woman with child at the shore,

& the barges at our part of the Narrows came back empty & singing

the way a dead tree creaks in the wind, sways in unison
    among the rest.

A dream is the web without the spider,

    the soft snap of rot—still so real to me, in a pristine ruin
    like her shower & the fogged glass

where we split a Pabst in the morning, before work, hungover,
    & trying to hold off the day.

The light doesn't hit my windows until noon now,

& quick as a razor across a stale Phille, memory flares with autumn's
    black leaves: vanished

cane-break: the pillars at the memorial in Berlin,

where I walked & she emerged & was gone in a peripheral
    & measured descent—a minnow sky

& children, with their elbows braced like a hen waiting to be clutched,
    played there. Hid.

    The city muffled their voices. The memorial muffles Berlin.

At a café table—*even the dead are dying.*

But the sky above my childhood home, edging down the hill,
    is a painting I carry, cast in a cheap gold frame,
    to every room I've lived in since.

    I came to art when I found myself in a dark wood, early in life,

because those years are like a house already sold, the furniture gone
    & the new picture frames not yet nailed to the walls—

what remains: there were lives in those rooms & there are lives there no more,
    like this summer, when I drove past the summers spent

32   drinking in a Little League diamond, John in the distance
       waving his phone to make trail marks in the outfield,

& Mike, next to me on the guitar, whose voice is still in the air there,
the way sometimes I believe

I've always been asleep on a long ride home.

Let the earth do what it will—

have me, spin the spokes until my memory fades to a ruthless spring.

God of War

Hummingbird, colibrí,
Huitzilopochtli
beats furious wings,
pushes heart to the brink
to feed on fermented sunrays
gathered in a flower's funnel.

Diminutive powerhouse,
you surveil your territory
from an obscured perch in a tree,
charge at trespassers
with staccato tweets,
your curved, stabbing beak.
Confidence rooted in speed,
the ability to cut through breeze.

Mouse-strong.
Snake-quick.
Eggs the size
of July acorns,
or foil-wrapped
Easter candy.

When my steps
disturb your nest,
I am glad
you are so small,

but your rage,
Huitzilopochtli,
forever haunts my dreams.

Survivor's Guilt: A Villanelle

for the family members of the incarcerated

> *You're a Caribbean woman. You cannot be without tribe.*
> —Willie Perdomo

I can only whisper this to you:
I've been called a survivor. It's a lie.
I've died 2,920 times. It's the truth.

I reanimate in Sing Sing, visiting siblings—play it cool.
I bury my heart—my mouth, the tomb. Gagging on life,
I can only whisper this to you.

I murder through suicide the girl of my youth:
I can't bear her nostalgia. For each day they serve time,
I've died 8,395 times. It's the truth.

I pretend it's okay; they pretend too.
I survived nothing. Can't speak aloud—I tried.
I can only whisper this to you.

I can't cry at goodbyes. *Don't make it worse*: Mother's rule.
I can't avoid home, pop pills, fly high. Without my tribe,
I've died 13,140 times. It's the truth.

Visit prisons gripping guilt like a bouquet of bloodroot.
Missed calls, unsent birthday cards, holidays are so cruel.
This can only be whispered to you:
We are dying. No one survives this. It's the truth.

Daydream

i'm walking down a street in mendoza. or what i remember of the street. the houses pressed tight together. each a flash of color. i can speak spanish. their spanish. as though my tongue and i grew up here. but i am still a me that exists because i grew up anywhere but here. pressed tight in these houses. each wall another's wall. no gap in between.

i go to her door. i knock. i wait. the door opens slightly. she peeks around it. scrutinizes me and my who / why / what i want. i ask if she's paying too much for her cable. she doesn't smell her own blood in front of her. it does not cross her mind that a twelve-year-old girl could come to this: fat / queer / not a girl.

the door closes. i keep walking. i swagger like my hips know this cement. same way the soft *jhe* always makes its way into *calle*. asphalt made sand by my molars. tender as the tip of my tongue to my back teeth. the lisp written into my genetics. like the fat and / queer and / not a girl.

my mom asks about abuela. i tell her: we drank mate. we had a lovely time. she only had nice things to say.

the relief in her smile becomes my language. becomes our blood.

Chivo Liniero

trenta libras de chivo six heinehquens one & a half bottles of broogahl añejo cinco puños de oregano & three hours later tía has tenderized the meat as a liniera she knows the exact amount of alcohol to add knowing too well what liquor does to a body during the time it takes for the stew to be ready to be consumed her eyes will monitor the flaming intensity created by multiple sources of heat   you see   mujeres linieras like my tía make chivo for special occasions over there the chivos are pre-seasoned lives sold on the pista hacia castañuelas at the crossroads of towns leading to ayiti in that hot sahara like part of the country goats are raised eating oregano while they are witnessing the movement chase displacement chase relocation chase trafficking capturing & slaughtering of the human world here I see tía take the bottle of dark rum aged in oak barrels deriving from molasses that are distilled from caña cut down by dark dominican hands some insist on calling ayitianos being born in living in & working in dominican bateyes tía removes la mayita & I want this netted cord to be the hamaca en que me tomo una siesta instead la mayita insists on being the net trapping my family's bottled up dominican american dreams I hear the clú, clú, clú of the caramel colored rum as it seeps into the meat able to resolver the taste of chivo as it's masticated rubs onto our tongues & dances between our cheeks tía ehplíqueme se dice que el que toma broogahl o resuelve o pelea but what is said about those of us who eat it is it responsible for the loving punch of my tone this chivo made mostly for gatherings of rebirth baby showers birthdays or año nuevo welcoming a new chapter of our family not having to endure the tutelage of el jefe el chivo supremo with every chivo cooked our family's history is recalled like the number of fincas y parcelas owned worked & that had to be sold trenta libras de chivo six heinehquens one & a half bottles of broogahl añejo cinco puños de oregano & thirty years later

thirty years later
in our family
there is still
so much
movement
chase
displacement
chase
relocation

& I don't
want to go
tía
in the Bronx
I want to stay.

Doña Teresa & the Chicken

the wooden house in Castañer didn't come with an air
conditioner or anything cool. The heat was its own
kind of music & so was abuela—demanding,
sharp-tongued. The kind of woman (I imagine)
whose teeth grew in because she told them to, so
the chicken never had a chance. It ran around
the backyard, flapping it's black-feathered wings
for mercy, for god's
attention, but Papá Dios knew better
than to get in between a chicken and a woman
feeding her grandkids. I looked over
my shoulder & there she was
chasing him, like an old lover
she came back to haunt, yelling,
¡hijo de puta! sin vergüenza! ven acá!
Her rosary beads slapped against her chest
over & over like a chant & you knew everything
in her path was temporary. Even the wind
buckled at the knees, at the sight of a woman
too wise to act like her blood was softer
than it was—& I saw her do it . . . & I think she knew,
because the chicken clucked so hard it spit up
its own good throat & she laughed, grabbed it
by the neck & swung it high above her
head like a propeller. Once, she gutted mom's
favorite pig with a machete & fed it to her
on her twelfth birthday. & maybe that's how mama learned
to love us: to kill the thing that feeds you.

Years later, she didn't go to her best friend's funeral or
the funeral of the vecina who mothered her in New York—barely
made it through abuela's. I suppose all she had was to love
until death & no more. So when we saw Doña Teresa lying
in the casket—arms crossed, chin cocked up—the whole family
cried & clawed, wanting her

to come back, wanting her to shout,
Didn't I prepare you better   than this—

Poems for Lelia

1.
In my mother's kitchen,
you're lucky if you have free reign of the refrigerator,
slightly colder than lukewarm and always in constant need of repair. Here,
my mother tells you where she keeps what
to make sure it doesn't rot:
>   the milk in the bottom-most shelf of the freezer.
>   the cheese in the crisp-produce drawer.
>   the chicken abandoned in the basement icebox.

Once an outdoor back porch covered in grapevines,
now an extension on stilts making space for a full-size oven.
A risky renovation unbeknownst and unapproved by the city. And just like that:
home out of thin air.

When my sisters and I laugh at the ways we have to
keep the water lightly running all winter
so the bare pipes below us don't burst,
or have to keep the kitchen
door ajar so the whole house doesn't fog,
she says, "Girls,"
with an accent thicker than the insulation of the floor beneath us,

"all my life, all I've ever wanted was a home
with a few flowers and a small plot of land.
And look—
look where you're standing."

2.
Lelia is a woman of routine.
She speaks to us through her practice,
her rhythms,
her permissions, and her *quítate de allí*.
She speaks to us in what she does and does not allow.

No instruction when she cooks,

just *espérate,*
give that back. You're doing it wrong.
In whose home can we afford to burn the carne?
We learn no lesson
is worth the hunger.

There are no second chances
for you, or apologies from her.
Just a silence sewing up our tongues before we could unravel our mouths.

We were a home of no repeated mistake.
Daughters of you gon' learn the first time.
No direction given, only taken.

She raised a pride of lionesses.
We study before we hunt.
We track before we touch.

When I am asked why I am so careful,
or why the calculation takes so long,
my only answer is my mother
raised us to know some women
don't have the luxury of fucking
up the first time.

We are her pride.

3.
Ever since my mother planted herself here,
she's had this thing with gardening.
She grows the unlikeliest flower
and somehow keeps it alive.

There is something about a woman who never lets a seed die,
who knows how to prune enough to grow things tall.

Although pruning has never made sense to me,
she understands it so well:
cut and slice and chop off the pieces
that just might die,
bloom faster, wider, stronger.

My mother is the type of woman who may not know the latest technologies of
   compost
but throws all her used peels
in the small patch of dirt known as her yard.
She may not have method to it,
but she knows that dead things make for rich soil
and she's bubbling over with roots she has to ground somewhere.

I wonder what border she thought she was crossing.
I wonder if she knew her skin held her own and only honey,
a sweetness to feed us all.

I wonder if she knew
when she traded continents
how much of a home she would make with her own hands,
how Brown girls are beautiful but not lovely,
how much she would have to cross, and sweeten, and bury, and plant, and
   prune, and let die
and let die
and let die
just to stay alive.

PoEma for MaMi

Mujer,

I picked this pen / up / from where you left it / on that wooden
desk / in a town you will learn to hate / you that
city girl / not that india sucia from Jutiapa / you would call yourself / you
only knew how to write your simple name / in all orders of /
UpPPercase AnD LoweRcase letters / and sometimes baby
cursive / that you managed to learn on your own //

you / a vieja / with abandoned school on your fingertips / I would
walk into classrooms with your signed forms / to scrunched
eyebrows / come-hither index fingers / pointing to the juxtaposing
signatures that were the wrong sizes for our bodies / your name /

mine //

sign here young lady / so I signed / to prove how well-colonized
I was / my perfect big-woman Oxford-English cursive / up against /
your toppling letters / a majestic view of uneven rooftops /
of the skyscrapers of a city that will become your first place of

many deaths //

my name is on your death certificate now / typed / below your
coffin six feet under your name /
the sole witness / the purveyor of truths / I don't know what I'll
write from here on / other than to remember to write the entire
alphabet / every time I write your name / spelling out all the
proverbs and the dichos that didn't die with you / setting those
concrete buildings on fire / creating

a new city of angels //

Ode to the Peacock

In the language of handkerchiefs // there's really nothing // I don't want
I'm glad to be paid in gold // when the devil beats his // you know what

if you think it's indecent // for a body to fan open iridescent // gird your gaze
because honey I'm throwing up // my kerchief like a flare-gun shot // watch me

unskirt a frosted muffin // top me with sprinkles // I'm flashing red-yellow-green go
you're the stallion and I'm the mare // smear my queer into the mirror // now you

are the mare and I am // the stale smell in the restroom stall // and you're an all-
you-can-eat buffet // let me say your eyes are the most beautiful // urinal cake blue

blew as in the past tense of blow // blow as in coke even though you // suck it up
buttercup and butterscotch // a man named Scott wants his scotch // filthy gorgeous

or maybe that's a martini // a man named Martin a man named // who knows what
who knows what it means to pluck roses // from my chest // using just his teeth

and sometimes yes blood // which is thicker than water // I know something thicker
it's called incest // when a nephew makes his uncle say uncle // say pee say cock

Katie Perry sings the song // let me see your peacock-cock // behold my royal flesh
stamped with eyes // don't tiptoe in your slippers // stomp on egg shells balloons

lick my boots until I see myself // being spit on like // you're squelching the inferno
sometimes fire sometimes feathers // elect a whip or bind me // blind in leather

pink polka-dot and seafoam green // if you don't already know // let me show you
what it means for a boy to be // a boy-to-be // when hard in my harness you'd best

call me daddy // but don't call any of this dirty // not unless the person doing it wants it
then it's smut // wipe the rosary from my brow // use the fabric pouring from your lips

Ode to the Chola

you wear attitude on your
brown-lined lips
spitting *fuck you* out
to the universe, not
owing it anything
but rolled eyes
and a sly smile.
you know something
that no one else does.
you hold the weight
of expectations
on your earlobes, those
gold hoops glittering
like halos above a
slicked-back ponytail.
you look at the mirror
like canvas, and you—
its art. *should be*
doesn't exist here
in the fabric
of the chola,
no *be more like*
no *be less like,*
just the steady beat
of a bass-heavy song,
of *tu corazón,*

i am, i am, i am.

December

Every year around December you come back to me in dreams, except you're a man now, tall like your father, dark like your mother, with a fly Miami accent and a low fade, an amateur boxer with a dope left hook, the king of blacktop ballers, tattooed and lean-muscled and sweaty, a barrio legend with a boy of your own, and sometimes you can't believe just how much your boy looks like and moves like the boy you were, and how you wish I was still around so you could say, *Look at my boy, Nena, just like Papi,* and brag about your identical jump shots. And every December I wonder if you've told him about our nights, reckless and faded and full of music, how you wrote all those lyrics about growing up poor and Afro-Rican and fatherless, how we took the streets, terrorized the neighborhood, and maybe there are tears in your eyes, and maybe there aren't, when you tell him how you loved me, how I loved you, how that was not enough, how when the holidays come around and the whole hood is blasting those aguinaldos and "Mi Burrito Sabanero," you remember those two kids we were, how we lied to each other, promised to be together forever because we didn't know any better, because we were only fourteen, because we needed to believe that there was someone.

My Uncle's Killer

wipes spots of toothpaste from the bathroom mirror
he shares nightly with his son. There, he's humanized,

again, in my imagination which keeps endowing him
with other forms: a lion with a bullet in its teeth;

a scythe-shaped smile on a child's back. Can I tell you
that, sometimes, I utter the word *justice* and mean *revenge*?

On my best nights, I mean *mercy*, but my best
is my rarest form. The figure of my uncle's blood

on the pavement, lit faintly by a gas station sign,
never changes. It's always, in my imagination, that same

dark isthmus connecting his body to the storm drain.
It floods in this town every year. In the last flood,

several coffins escaped their graves to the horror
of almost everyone. I, though, am glad to see the past intrude

as spectacle, an image that refuses our forgetfulness
as captivation. Freedom, after all,

is what binds me to the worst version of myself.
Shout *freedom*. You can't help it. You've made a threat.

Poem in Consideration of My Death
after Vallejo

I will die on Sunday afternoon in Saginaw
following a plate of my mother's
enchiladas, fried chicken, and rice.
I will scrape up the congealed queso fresco
and sauce with a tortilla chip, with my
index finger among the garnish of iceberg
lettuce and chopped tomato.
Full, I pour a cup of coffee.
My father is there in his 1986 blue Buick Regal.
If there is a heaven this is it—
the car lot on State Street, my father's smile
as we discuss the different shades of red: candy, burgundy,
cherry, and something that sparkles in between.
I know I am dead as we drive to pick up tortillas,
the last stop every Sunday.
The day will slice itself into a lemon,
splay its fingers and clean the salt
from its nails as we roll our tortillas
on Grandma Rico's porch made of red tulips.
We cannot eat in the car.
The sun setting is her gold tooth, beyond the
abandoned parking lot covered in dandelions.
If I could fold one flower in half and pluck
the creased eyes of a petal, I would know
what it means to pause before that space
where earth meets the lens of my eye upside down
when my father hands me the keys still warm from his pocket.
The salt and sour of the lemon my, final taste of this planet.
My mother will gather her blue robe,
line it with roses, cut like stars.

Dandelion Graves

Kids of the forgotten refugees, soilless seeds
On the run from the barrel of a gun, on their knees
Ducking immigration until they're stationed as far as DC
Or LA or the bay, that was back in Reagan's 80s
When numbers shot up like a fiend, crack rock was being steamed
In the apartment down the hallway from my mama's baby
But that wasn't the home that my parents made for me
Georgia Ave and Urbana in lily-white Montgomery
Except the Glenmont section was Brown as Abuela's coffee
And the smell of asphalt would never wash off Papi
A good day was a meal that wasn't frijoles and cheese
So my dreams were drenched in leftover Chinese
But pull yourself and you'll succeed is the bullshit they would feed
So everyone drank piss until they couldn't see
Cuz how's a kid like me supposed to think when it's engraved
The only future that awaits is a dandelion grave

Her Arms Filled with Stars

I am not going to die, I'm going home like a shooting star.
—Sojourner Truth

I. Northampton, Massachusetts, 1843

Born stolen, under an unfamiliar name,
she shuffled the letters, apellido
became Truth, her question
uncomplicated

        ¿Qué no soy yo mujer?

To sojourn, me voy
a quedar un rato, don't take
your shoes off, don't unpack

Storm swirling up through
the maze of bones on her back,
pushing limbs up each morning
She looked the gusts in the eye,
pulled it out from the center

        ¿Qué no soy yo mujer?

On fire, a form you can't decipher,
disposable in its invisibility,
un pedazo de algo se está
quemando, someone tied
the extremities,
to burn her

Bold font of news blurb detailed
debris in flames, in the silhouette
of a woman's body

Embers extending over epidermis
bloomed orange petals, sparked
the red of spirit wanting to unfold
wings tucked under a woman's arms

The flames didn't release the trunk
of her exhalation, skin dried like a discarded
husk in limbo, her family asking

¿Qué no es ella mujer?

III. Rio Bravo, Texas, 2018

One third of a mile from braided wire
and blistered lines in the sand, the border patrol
agent plucked her young life from her, the dyes
in her woven skirt suffocated in an overgrown
lot, her last breaths releasing the fire fronds

of azaleas, a metamorphosis of girl and blossom,
into scaled appendage, the people asking

¿Qué no es ella mujer?

The eruption royal orange
winged insects in transit before
the clawed butterfly holds court when
the scourge of our skin the question
remaining, of mercy and flesh, the question

        ¿Qué no somos?
        ¿Qué no somos?
        ¿Qué no somos?

This poem was part of an installation in the 2018 Day of the Dead Exhibit at the Mission Cultural Center in San Francisco: *Flight of the Ancestors*. This poem forms part of the art piece entitled, *¿Qué no soy yo mujer?* by Evelyn Orantes and Leticia Hernández-Linares. Our multimedia installation remembers Claudia Patricia Gómez Gonzáles, a Mayan woman murdered by a federal border agent in Texas in May 2018, and pays homage to the countless Black, Brown and Trans women who have been killed because of dominant culture's treatment of our bodies as disposable. We honor the transformation of women's bodies into resilient, winged spirit-warriors accessing their ultimate power. We must continue to resist this violence, and we also look to our ancestral beliefs to help us understand the light beyond our corporal bodies.

For the Record

I scan the list of names
in the *in memoriam* columns
billowing bits of star
and old rivers, think I grasp
what the concept of time
truly steals from us.
Then dinner, the dishes
a moment given
to write with invisible ink.

The Tempest

My father decided I would be born at sea,
Thirsty & surrounded by the risk of drowning

My father was a great sailor, a seaman, navigated
Only the darkest waters—the sweetest squalls

Which is to say he was a drunk, like his father
Before him, & now I had to learn the rhythm of the waves

How a full moon makes water bulge, makes high & low tide
I had to learn to follow stars home, to strange ports

My father decided I would be born at sea
So he left me in a dugout—the shoreline nowhere in sight

Thank God for the saints—those monoliths on land,
Light towers on the sea & eagles in the sky

Which is to say thank God for mamás, tías, & abuelas
Where would the wandering sailor babies float to without them

Blesséd be these lights who did their own time on the sea,
Who enjoyed a storm or two before the warm hearth of a slick boatsman

Who pay their penance as watchers of the sailor's bastards
Who drink tears & listen to boleros on Friday & Saturday nights

& yell and scream at us as if we were those lost sailors
& apologize & console us as if we were those lost sailors

Títere Ring

ghosts fit loose on the finger

                              holy broken bodies by a solemn fire
            island more than just fragments of memory or imagination

men gather tentatively at the corner
                        desolate cuchifritoes of the mind
                        speak the eternity beyond you in gauzy sapphires
                              speaking of survival & the precious things
                                                            unkept

purple sunsets along avenue c   our ancestry
                              signified
                              impressionistic genocide

      men gather tentatively at the corner   prayers rounded back again
                                                beads of tears & bacardi
                                                gathered in red threads
what's true or not isn't important   what is felt

            heart pouched in gray palms for too long
                              purpled afternoon bruises
                                          the time papi left home
                                                      & came home
                                                            drunk
sun rises and sets still
                  sons cross the last green horizons   men
                                                                  drunk
                                                      on sound
                                                      on voices
                                                      on laughter
a chord holds on orange fire pits
                  lined against the skull   meditation worth something

      burnt & balanced on a shadow   bachata salsa bolero jazz

old poets find their books in concrete
a ceaseless playing
an intersection of mental ends
a ceaseless search for meaning

mythology broken more than once

men gather tentatively at the corner

under searchlights & streetlights

without a cycle of birth
death
afterlife

worn sometimes without warning

we won't want the world to shake
but to finally come to rest
papers out of every pocket
song on every tongue
in tongues
holyed   someday
ourselves into puro breath
puro voice
puro patria   free
free
libre

Fellowship Application

PLEASE PROVIDE AN INTRODUCTION TO YOUR WORK
(250 WORDS)

RESPONSE:

MY POETRY COMES from a big water truck bouncing
and exhaling smoke over dry molds of wheel marks
made by other trucks that passed the same way sometime
last season at the same packinghouse in a different no-
stoplight, Central California town with another name that
will be mispronounced in perpetuity, which is to say forever, as
ever and this error will be defended until it is
deemed correct and most true. Amen. Amén. Ah, men.
This is the poetry of a man in the passenger seat of said
truck. He's trying to light a cigarette amidst all the
vibrations and the damn truck keeps moving. Chewy is
talking again. I gotta get his words on the page, but this
match keeps blowing out. These poems, though, they
wanna be about something beautiful like birds 'n' shit.
Chewy keeps talking about birds. One hand on the
wheel, he leans forward to look up and from under his
cap. His other hand enters my space with fingers out like
he's flying or the birds are flying or we're flying or the
truck is flying; we're birds now and I still can't get this
shit lit. The water treatment plant is an entire ecosystem
of migratory birds, he says. This poetry is for the birds. It
wasn't until my third week at work that I realized me and
Chewy are probably cousins. Some border crossing
mess, a case of mistaken identity, papers and names on
paper. It only counts if it's on paper. Unfamiliar words
that don't match faces. I could quote Borges again, but
I'll chill. FYI, I just went over the word cap. Somebody
baptized their first cousin and, like me, didn't realize it.
Grandma's porchside pre-9/11 mention is the only living
artifact. Art-is-fact? Art are facts. The packinghouse is
full of abuelas. Full of art-are-facts. All forthcoming

58   poetry will attempt to revive dead abuelas and their art-
is-facts. One of those decolonized sisters told me this
hummingbird was my abuela. Okay, I'm wit' that.
Henceforth, all abuelas are hummingbirds. Poetry should
be full of abuelas, full of birds, full of birds who take you
to the doctor and tell your teacher you got diarrhea so
don't trip if he asks to go to the bathroom more than
once. Full of birds who know why you're passed out on
the living room floor but still make you eggs and papas
in the afternoon. Birds! Who scrapbooked all your
articles in the local paper about Division II softball and
community college wrestling. Full of birds! Old birds too
busy dirty-packing muscat and wonderfuls. Birds that get
cancer. Birds that get valley fever. Birds that die of
diabetes. Birds that watch professional wrestling and
own cats with feline leukemia. I hate that my poetry has
to be about this shit, but it's true, Bill Moyers. It's true,
Harold Bloom. I'm not making it up, Don Share. I see
you over there, Tom Lutz. The rivers in these poems got
arsenic in 'em and not in the funny, Cary Grant way.
More like the bye-bye-Tía-Cissy way, bye-bye-Chicana-Role-
Model, bye-bye-Iceworker, bye-bye-Tía-Cookie, and
bye-bye-Coach-Garza kinda way, wey. And each and every
night, I'll write you faithfully. All of you. When we die, I
hope we all go to the bird's nest built by ese Ai Weiwei.
And maybe then I'll stop telling this tired-ass story. But
anyway, Chewy says I gotta go back to work now, and I
finally got this cigarette going. Jesús had a lighter the
whole time, that bastard. I'll tell you this, ain't nothin' in
this whole world like blowing smoke in the middle of a
newly plowed field like this one. Punto. Neta. Bye.

We Is
In conversation with the work of Wilfredo Valladares and Ayo Ngozi

We is not the singular
dotted i, black figure against
white background.

We is the crowd
that moves into this dance
of morning rituals,
this waking to the rooster crow
of a city.

We is the dance
that shakes and rolls
down city streets,
shimmies into markets
for fresh fruit,
salsas against traffic.

We is the traffic
rushing past the living
and the dead
forgetting to write our songs down,
breathe into Chinese-medicine bottles
so we can heal the wounds
of our entrances and exits.

We is the song of migration
sung from behind the masks—
fragile resin, cast from faces
whose eyes must remain
closed so their pasts
do not pour from them,
their present does not
burn away home.

We is home

60 carried into conversation,
    about a crowing rooster,
    a ritual, dancing, and medicine
    to cure what ails us.

Parable of the Mustard Seed

The destiny of Earthseed is to take root among the stars.
—Octavia Butler

When they drilled through our homes for the six hundredth genocide,
and the machines they built turned the dirt to tar
and made the air unbreathable,
my ma turned to me and said,
"Ven aqui. Tell everyone.
It is time to go."
And when we walked out of our apartment building,
everyone was already there.
My cousin Chico
and his son who did the best tattoos;
Beli and Mari,
sisters who played in a band
and had lived across from us since I was four;
even the couple who fought all night,
who sometimes I would imagine were seals
on some beach so I could sleep.
They were all there,
ready to take off.

Of course, that is the reason
there are little to no Black, Brown, queer, trans bodies
in so many science fiction movies.
It's not about whose life is valued
enough to be shared on a big screen.
We are not in their stories *anymore*
because we left.

And no,
it is not because they have finally succeeded in killing us.
When they took away healthcare,
we came together and cared for each other,
looted the pharmaceutical stores,
built our own hospitals out of one another's apartments.
When their state-sanctioned bullies tried to murder us,

62 we made mirrors of our bodies,
    reflected the bullets back.
    We showed up and showed up
    until we were never alone.

    This is our story
    of blue-flower abuelas selling chicle and tamales on our front porches,
    of valuing the work of our hands and our hearts,
    even if and because no one else would.
    And I will tell you
    that it was good for a time
    on Earth,
    when there was still food
    to feed ourselves
    and clean water.
    But our destiny
    has always been to take root
    among the stars.

    When we first left,
    the bigots cheered, *it took them long enough.*
    Said, *this is our great nation again,*
    even as it turned to ash beneath their greed.
    And what a sad world they were left
    without our spices, our sweet lotions and loud laughs,
    our thick bodies and poetry.

    Some of them
    say they saw us leave:
    a great flood of bodies
    lifting themselves off the ground,
    together
    a flock of birds.
    They must have thought
    it was a mass suicide.
    They must not have known
    we could fly.

    Arms linked,
    not one of us
    looked back.

17

El Bandolon

Afro-Colossus (A Hip-Hop Cento)

Let me loosen up my bra strap,
conquering limbs astride
from land to land, check it
how I rock it, this
Mother of Exiles.

Big-body girl that's kickin' it.
Send these: the homeless,
tempest-tossed to me—
I consume the room
or the moon,

not like the brazen giant
of Greek fame,
rage in effect
so now
ya know.

Here at our sea-washed, sunset
gates shall stand
a mighty woman with a torch
whose flame
I rock.
It's the Lady
of Rage still
kicking up
dust.

The wretched refuse
your teeming shore.
Rock on
with your
bad
self.

I lift my lamp

rock rough
with my bad self,

with my   Afro,
with my   Afro,
with my   Afro,

beacon-hand.

I rock rough,
I rock rough,
I rock rough,
with my
(rage!)

Sources: Lady of Rage, "Afro-Puffs;" "The New Colossus," Emma Lazarus

Petition to Get All White Girls to Stop Wearing Hoop Earrings

There's a petition to get all white girls to stop
wearing hoop earrings. I didn't know this was a thing
except when I thought about it
being a thing, like when I rejected
my hoops in my backpack once in the middle of the school day
because I thought I heard someone say a slur I was
sure was over. My lover told me about this. Showed me
the article. The comments. The thread. He has big holes
in his ears left over from gauges. They're in
the shape of little screaming mouths.
These are silly, I'd say. *These are fun.*
Last summer he threw the earrings into the ocean
because, he told me, *white people ruin everything.*
Even though all the girls he chose
to really love are named Lauren or Hailey.
I say this like my name isn't Melissa.
Like my name couldn't wrap itself securely around
Lauren's neck. Or Hailey's wrists.
Like it couldn't slide itself neatly through
any of their earlobes and hang there all day,
belonging

Eddie Guerrero Enters a Ring Holding the World Championship

the body brown, belt gold, eyes closed, nose in the air,
shoulders shake to each word: i lie, i cheat, i steal.

white men, what you hold sacred we will take: money, cars,
liquor, land, life, winning. you won't like this. that's fine.

our world champion drives bouncing low lows, talks shit.
he: grins through crimson masks, slit roaring red, red rain;

lifts bodies into orbit, drops them like judgments;
leaps from turnbuckles, bronze fist blooming into flames.

brown bodies know that violence is the marriage
between their hot ambition and the rule of law.

what respect can we have for the word "legal" since
"illegal" can describe our skin, our joy, our life?

i lie, i cheat, i steal. i lie, i cheat, i steal.
our champion of the world pokes eyes, low-blows, spits.

behind the ref's back, he hits the floor with a chair
(metal clang), chucks it into his opponent's hands,

collapses as though shot. the ref turns around, shocked.
he points to his white foe, gets him disqualified.

there's no difference between a fair win and a win
except how much your faith in the system frees you.

what good are your rules if they grant only your dignity?
what good are your codes if broken by our breathing?

68   our world champion struts over a white body.
      we're not meant to exist with such extravagance.

      i lie, i cheat, i steal. we lie, we cheat, we steal.
      smile with your tongue out in celebration of broken laws.

On Bombing

10.

Nineties kids called whatever we admired *the bomb*.

9.

When no one laughs at a comedian's jokes, we say he bombed.
If the comedian inspires peals of laughter, we say he killed
tonight, or she knocked them dead. The act of killing creates
regurgitation of noise, the slayed leave satisfied, while

the defining characteristic of bombing is callous silence. Is
the distinction a matter of timing, of rhythm? Is the dying
dependent on creating a conducive environment? Or is it
about complicity? When the crowd rejects the comedian's

joke there is fallout without detonation, the dissatisfaction
crushing the room's morale. If the joke solves Mark Twain's
equation of humor equals tragedy plus time, the laughter
will become pandemic, and the comic lays claim to the kill.

8.

Bombing in comedy is usually due to one
or more of the following factors: the word choice is stale,

the comic's timing and tone are asynchronous, their point
of view trite or overused. And Twain's equation is not duly

employed. Perhaps there was tragedy but the timing was off,
or tragedy was not employed with wit and grace. Some jokes

are *too soon*, others are insensitive to the audience's world
view. It is possible that the comic misread the room, was *tone-
deaf* in their delivery. Without proper execution of these

elements the comic misfires and the joke does not land,

as they say in the business. It was a dud. The joke is unable
to light the fuse of the limbic system, thus no guffaw erupts.

If after discharging a joke only coughing and the clack of pint
    glasses can be heard, the comic is marooned, left alone on

stage to wonder if this will be their last gig. It didn't land.
                                                    They bombed.

7.

In 1950, American jet fighters struck the towns of Jayuya
and Utuado. It was one of two occasions in which the US
bombed its own citizens. Apparently, some Puerto Ricans

were not thrilled about being occupied, so they organized
a rebellion to expel the invaders. In response to the staged
insurrection, the foreign sovereign bombed civilians. Now

if one were to make the analogy that the foreign sovereign
is to the island as the comic is to the club, then the imposed
citizenship is a joke that did not land, and the rebellion is equal

to heckling the comic. The hack foreign sovereign hates being
heckled, cannot tolerate having bombed, so they opened fire.
The bombing of the cities was a surprise. Surprise has long

been a trusted tool of the comic. It can be applied by exploiting
the ambiguity of a word or phrase, by abruptly shifting a story's
focus. The trick is to challenge your audience's expectations.

Here, no one expected they would bomb civilians. This one
landed. The hecklers were silenced. It was tragedy. Plus time.
Whereas with comedy, both comic and crowd are pleased when

the joke lands, this form of bombing leaves only the bomber
sated. Leaves only the bomber. The bomb lands. The crowd
demands their money back. But there will be no refund.

On Fordham road, two kings are busted for bombing

      the Family Welcome Center. Their black and purple

throwie reads, *Life B 4 Cash*. The court will frame them

      as felons, but their bombing is just impersonation

of the forefathers, the original tag-bangers who

      slammed the Six Grandfathers—hallowed terrain

of the Lakota, the Cheyenne, the Arapaho, the Kiowa—

      with a colossal burner of granite and mica schist

plugging Washington, Jefferson, Roosevelt, Lincoln.

    5.

The former bomb is a joke that didn't land, landing
the kids on probation. The latter bomb is a desecration
of land, a silence bolstered by shrapnel of tourism.
The bomb was seen as a joke to some, though it isn't

    4.

                  exactly funny.

    3.

Graffers bomb to exert their right to create, to reclaim
grifted territory. If you say you bombed the J train, your
claim has two concurrent meanings: first, it means you
branded the train, and thus the landscape, with your
personal style, so the train belongs to you, at least
until the city cleans the train or another writer bombs
your piece. Second, it means that you have beautified
a space that was intentionally made ugly by private

72   interests. So, you see, bombing is both an act of sedition
      and addition. When graffers bomb the surface
      of a thing, they are planting begonias in an ash heap.

          2.

      An antipode to when Clinton bombed Kosovo,
      or when Bush bombed Iraq, or when Obama
                          bombed Yemen, or when Reagan bombed
                          Beirut, or when Nixon bombed Cambodia,
                          or when Eisenhower bombed North Korea,

      or when Truman bombed Japan, or when
      Trump bombed Syria. Those bombings
      did not beautify, resurrect, or give birth,
      though the bombers were aiming to lay claim
      over a territory in an inversion of what graffers

          call *going all-city.*

          1.

      When comics bomb, the silence
      it engenders is followed by yawning.

      When graffiti writers bomb, the silence
      it engenders is followed by awe

      (or a summons). When fighter
      planes bomb, the

          0.

          -1.

      *(Multivalent in its application, the single common characteristic of bombing is that in all
      scenarios the act is perceived to be an endpoint in, or interruption to, a charted course, a
      proposed solution to a lack: of imagination, of resources, of joy. Both the bomber and the bombed
      now inextricably coupled.*

                                          Both permanently altered.)

Afro-Latinx Manifesto
(or I Learned to Count Salsa Steps
to Laffy Taffy by D4L)

Summer '93. Mommy goes to have her thyroid checked and doesn't. Learns I'm on the way. Celia Cruz finds mommy in the street and kisses her stomach. Says *este niño es bendecido.* Pops tells me this to assure me I wasn't an accident. Pops left when I was eight months old. Pops would tell people he raised me well. Trust when I say not to trust Pops, and as his son, trust when I say I ran from my family like Pops. I said no to whatever Abuela Ana tried putting on my plate. Mommy never put anything on my plate; she was too busy working and going out and going out and finding the next place to be. Fell down a flight of steps as a baby. Mommy wasn't paying attention or was too busy. Pops found me at the bottom. Then something about knuckles and Mommy's ability to hide the way Pops loved her. Either way I was a baby so I was barely there. Then I grew up and Mommy and Pops were barely there but Celia Cruz kissed Mommy's stomach. Abuelo would brush his teeth and I was on the toilet imagining what heaven would be like. I was in the second grade and Ms. Young was tall and gave me poetry and taught me how to read the hands of a clock. Ms. Young was my first Black teacher and the first person who took their job of nurturing seriously, not for the check but for the hurt child she saw in me hiding in my love for Langston Hughes. In a river. I speak and say I'm hungry and I love you. I was an easy child with nothing at ease. Héctor Lavoe every Sunday and I could care less. I'm playing video games, or scooping out an extra cup of rice from a green drum so I can definitely have thirds but never concón. There's preference and then there's rejection. You see where I'm going? DC to eat my homey's mom's shrimp and grits for breakfast? Ushering in 2013 with jungle juice and Tio Mingo on life support. Dance-floor wet, supporting folk I never met while they got dubbed on. Swag surfed into another house party. The girls I came to the parties with became my sisters; our sweated-out clothes made us kin. We, holding each other up so bent that we was straight and it was all I needed. We were all we needed. A week later Abuelo dies visiting Tio Mingo the day he was taken off life support but we don't tell him anything. For once it's not pride that silences the family but loss and the inability to imagine heaven. Another week passes and Tio Mingo joins Abuelo for a double wake at Ortiz Funeral Home off 190th y Broadway. Fire hazard of grief spilling out the chapel. Enough cousins I never met to wonder how much easier it all could've been. Enough family to feel part of one. I let go of my father's abandonment to carry a name I knew better than any. Ramirez. I started hearing the music differently. Something muddled but mine. Something you couldn't tell me wasn't genetic like blood, like hips, like rhythm, like activism. I started carrying myself the way I needed to be carried as a baby, with love or what I would confuse for love. I let someone take my hands. El Día de mi Suerte. I move like I didn't need a translator. I sing with my whole heart like I picked fruits the island bore. Shouting *¡Azúcar!* Gap-toothed with a truth my family couldn't keep up with. *Este niño tiene tumbao.* I am them and Black at the same time.

¿Cómo es posible? De dónde es tu familia? Where not even death keeps us from dancing.

infinite wop
after Biz Markie's "Alone Again" and Jodie Foster in *Contact*

I will whip out
this stupid loneliness
it will slip
into the spinning rings
the blinding light
the wormhole
of my hip
my neck
my back

I am okay to go
into another
dimension
a vision of
vast idiocy
and solitude
release it
through my
otherly-abled limbs

this solo woe
will drop into
the Möbius strip
of my infinite wop
my idiot savant bop
and be transformed

a slowed forgetting
memory broken
and pieced
back together
by beat
body cracked dumb

I will hum

76   myself into a universe
     of un-aloneness
     and quadruple suns
     wind into
     never-before-seen
     galaxies
     while staying in
     one spot

     chat up
     an alien who looks
     like my father
     and points me
     to the single dancers
     on the floor
     in their own heads
     their own bodies
     each a cosmos
     alone until collision

     infinite wop (video instructions)

     copy and paste or click on
     or type in these URLs
     and open these two videos:

     Biz—"Alone Again"—http://youtu.be/OebqNsNRBtU
     Jodie—"Contact Space Travel"—https://youtu.be/scBY3cVyeyA

     pause Biz at beginning
     watch Jodie from beginning
     with volume on until :30
     pause and mute Jodie
     play Biz
     restart Jodie right away from :30 in
     and watch
     when song is done
     unmute or raise volume in Jodie
     and close Biz window
     watch end of Jodie

Everybody Loves Cardi B But

only if she *speak good*
only if she made it despite *speaking bad*
only if our daughters don't admire her
only if we can listen to her album on code switch
only if she gets woke
only if she makes us laugh
only if we pretend she's never cried
only if we can intellectualize the hood
only if we can point fingers at her and not patriarchy
only if we know how we are oppressed
only if we don't talk about how we are oppressing
only if we got a good job
only if we made "better" decisions than she did
only if people follow us for the right reasons
only if our poems sound like dissertations
only if our poems *speak good*
only if our poems make it despite *speaking bad*
only if our trauma has graduated college
only if she doesn't remind us of what we were told not to be
only if she doesn't remind us of what we've survived

La Llorona Watches the Movie *Troy*

She watches Brad Pitt leap, then land a stab
like a hammer blow, spends time taking in
the bronze skin of the actors, the way the say "grass"

like "toss," *¡Todo British!* She snags popcorn
by the handful watching the gods
be shrugged off by warriors. During the scene

where the Greeks scurry from the Trojan horse,
their shadows fingers pulling at string
and unraveling the night, her breath is sand

and crackling flame. When they run toward fire
in the desert, toward collapsing roofs
and digitized screaming, the montage

of faces, of bodies pushing against each other
has her whispering to no one in particular:
¡Mira Baghdad, mira Juárez! And no one

in particular hears her over the Dolby
of swords being unsheathed. She begins to hum,
letting her voice hit the same notes

as the opera singer overlaid during the carnage.
Should anyone look over, they'd see
the silhouette of a woman in the third row

treating the forty-foot screen like an altar.
When, after seeing the toppling of statues
and the scavenging through offerings

to Apollo, sun god, the one who sees everything,
the aged and fallen king staggers in defeat
and cries out: *Have you no honor!?*

Have you no honor!?, she gasps and nods,
as if watching a telenovela unfold
according to how she would want it. Truth is,
she has seen this all before, has drowned
the Brown bodies, has plucked gold coins
from river water before any boatman

could make his way to her. She knows
the blonde and blue-eyed have arrived
to play both hero and love interest again,

that though Helen here is a vagabond Marilyn,
she used to have *un poquito de chile*
in her blood, *y un puñado de lodo*

in her heart. That's why it's a woman
who says: *If killing is your only talent,*
then it is your curse, and says it

like one slapping their hand against the river,
a sting in their hands for a while. Truth is,
there will always be a Brad to leap and hit hard,

the thud through the speakers like a heartbeat.

And

Withstand pandemonium
and scandalous
nightstands
commanding candlelight

       and
        quicksand

and zinfandel
clandestine landmines
candy handfuls
and contraband

       and
        handmade

commandments
and merchandise
secondhand husbands
philandering

       and
        landless

and vandal
bandwagons slandered
and branded
handwritten reprimands

       and
        meander

on an island
landscaped with chandeliers
abandon handcuffs
standstills

                    and
                    backhands

notwithstanding
thousands of oleanders
and dandelions
handpicked

                    and
                    sandalwood

and mandrake
and random demands
the bystander
wanders

                    in
                    wonderland.

Fat Joe at the Ninth Grade Dance

my   niggas   don't   dance
we   just   pull   up   our   pants
and hug ourselves / when we are sure
no one else will / we cradle the gangly
architecture puberty left us / five feet
ten inches of ash and bone and the
most crisp white tees our mother's
ironing boards could conjure / fists
clenched around any bass line that
promises to swell / our sharp elbows
a suit of armor / cuz ever since Tai got
armpit hair and started flexing muscles
that even make the teachers look twice
/ ever since we grew taller than our
girlfriends and thought ourselves men /
ever since Maria got pregnant / and
Jeremy got his teeth kicked in / and we
saw them break like dice across the
school parking lot / ever since then /
my niggas don't smile / my niggas don't
dance / my niggas square up / my
niggas carve ulna and radius into sword
and shield / my niggas turn quiet
survival tactics cacophony each time we

lean back

The first two lines of this poem are borrowed from the Terror Squad's "Lean Back"

Ode to Kendrick Lamar

There are nights like tonight when it rains / biblical amounts of everything
and music plays while I drive somewhere I usually don't / go after dark
because I get lost in my head / while my wife plans for next week and I try
to decide / where to park and when to leave but instead I down / IPAs and
smash / burgers into my gut before the smallest words crawl / out, forced.
Some days I feel the dark rushing, a tidal wave of fuck / you's cresting
my insides. / I double-knot my Tims and avert eye contact in a hoodie
and baseball cap. / I am not / this facade, have never sailed a fist into a
stranger's / skull, but there is a thunderstorm / here and I must know my
way. Tomorrow / I will drive a pick-up to the end / of the road on the
other side of 880. I will park and read / poetry while 18-wheelers rumble
within inches of my chest. It is what excites / and repels my attention while
riding this / neighborhood. How the blood of sweet grass reminds me of
something else.

Apology to Her Majesty, Queen Cardi B
after Layli Long Soldier

Whereas Jimmy prolly can't pronounce
your name; whereas that green mink's

mad loud for primetime yuppies; whereas
pasty mugs quietly sipped the Bronx

in a canned Q&A; whereas tickle-me-
white, the color they blushed

after you hollered, *Eyyuum!*;
whereas was it with, or against you?

Whereas dey prolly ain't ever seen
homegirls wreathe you
as their patron saint—

lil' Lauras wit dey laurels,
whose mouths run the block

searing *chisme* over hot concrete
and toe straps; whereas blessed b

the scented velas of acetone and plugged-in irons,

and still you trill
the hymns of jainas;

you who told the limelight
Don't get too close cuz I ain't put

no lotion on my hands; whereas se ríen
as you explain your name, how Henny's

the suture of Black and Brown hands
who killed a forty for each hour

on the job, who lick wounds
with liquor's promise of numbness;

whereas the smh tías who gawk
at the peacock tat running your thighs,

and sigh, *cómo hemos caído*; whereas
that part in "Motorsport," where you bent

in front of butterfly doors, hollered,
I'm the trap Selena!; whereas the bark

that tickles my skin, as it does in the shade
when me and the fellas untuck

the gaze we've longed to spliff all week;
whereas errtime I aimed homeboy's head

like a slingshot, a young-woman-turned-
pair-of-legs passed through the quad,

and eyes carved into bare flesh;
whereas I chewed a human being

with a dangling mouth
and called her redbone, feigned

to stare at the dead men
she hefted; whereas I respected

the spine of a book, the tattered
cloth of hardcover,

more than her own;
whereas these temples of Hoteps

whet teeth with passed-down
stones, our crumbling masonry,

beret down plazas chanting
     freedom, yet in dorm parties

     bite off a brother's tongue,
     so he speaks nothing

     but our worst hungers;
     that snarl, *Who's the lookout*

     today?, as we try to out-smoke
     each other, for the dogs we is.

     May I catch the fang she spits
     back, chew on my own question:

     No, are you with or against?
     And I too am inside that studio,

     clapping with them.

     Therefore, be it resolved, Cardi,
     Queen of the Bronx, this apology:

     may the two-legged perros
     claw this gangrene out,

     so the tender vespers
     that flock our word

     do not recite our catechisms.
     May you and all the women

     who've guided my life
     never see the eyes

     I once hawked.

An Apology for Trashing Magazines in Which You Appear

I was out of line, Brad Pitt.
You're no Eliot Spitzer.
I'm no preacher. This apology no bully pulpit
where I sermonize our epitasis—
Woody Allen tragicomedy in which I play "Serendipity"
and am blinded by you, a star, Jupiter

(third brightest in the night, spitting
image of the sky god). *Patience* might be for pipits
and "forever" a spit
of land neighboring Atlantis, but I'll wait my turn. Pity
your first marriage ended. I didn't mind her as much as that Jolie-Pitt
situation, complete with pitter-

patter of twelve Benetton-inspired feet. But, I'm not bitter. My pit
bull bears your name, and I call my man—with whom I'm going to Pittsburgh
for a wedding—out his name, into yours: Brad Pitt.
Daydreams of you and me rivaled only by Brandon and me on *Peach Pit*
counters, from the original *90210*. Even so, I'd wish he were you. Adonis
    epitome.
Abandon Hollywood for Bed-Stuy, skip down spit-

paved sidewalks to my brownstone. My poetry pittance,
your movie money. . . I suspect we'd do fine with our combined capital.
We'd be the mixed-race Pitts
on Tompkins Park. I'd be hospitable,
hosting meet-and-greets so as not to appear uppity.
Casually introducing you, I'd say, "Oh, this is Brad. This is just Brad Pitt."

You'd find macabre humor in my obsession with Poe's "Pit
and the Pendulum" and the palpitating
"Tell-Tale Heart." The heart is an odd organ, a maudlin muscle, a cesspit
of undeserved affection. I admit I've had trouble pitting
good sense against non, but who hasn't? (Did you know the per capita

divorce rate is 50 percent? Pitiful.)

Like with Juliette and Jennifer, I pray Angelina was a pit
stop on your way to Brooklyn. When I first saw you, Brad Pitt,
I was fifteen and became so ill I was rushed to the hospital.
My hands, feet, and armpits
began to sweat as if I were riding horseback up a hill toward a love who made
    the pit
of my stomach ache; literally, *Legends of the Fall* was my pitfall.

Brad Pitt, I imagine a much older you—spitfire
and only slightly decrepit—staring my epitaph
down as if your gaze were the capital and my headstone a ghetto to be pitied.

1983 Oldsmobile

No problema, Jose trades his VCR and a gold chain
for a Cutlass Supreme, its body a shatter of paint,
rims more grime than shine, its motor a soup pot
of cylinders spilling, oil shellacking the blacktop streets.
A miracle in each ignition, we would roll, seats split,
the dashboard diced by sun in a hip-hop of exhaust.
Each bump and block of turns rocked us to a totter,
a ruckus of hydraulics, all pimped out with woofers
singing more hostage than siren, more hiss than MC.
Wu-Tang warbles with Method Man and Raekwon
trading lines on torture, spiked bats, and wire hangers.
And as I sit in Humanities 101, I dream of those rides
instead of discussing *The Prince* as my professor prompts
me to provide my own example of Machiavellian torture.

Poetics Lesson at the Baruch Houses

If homegirl's mama is a thirteenth floor bochinchera,
   will the line break between platano and relleno
   remove the wrought iron from her playground?

Watch this block simmer with thieves and curly-headed babies
   that look like you.
Watch the cops circle this block in search of thieves and babies
   that look like you.
Offer the kindly officer your ass to kiss.
Stand in the "No Standing" zone.

Nothing about you says ghetto or housing project,
but you love it when Biggie makes mothafuckas take dirt naps
   in poems where you didn't realize
   that dime sacks were not really ten cents.

Homegirl packs your car with beauty products and baby clothes.
This is cliché to the critic from the *New York Times*.
This is cache to the Boricua studies professor.
"Motherfucker!" homegirl says. "I just wanted to say that.
   You seemed to be deep in thought, and I love interrupting you
   when you are deep in thought."

Here is the turn: the bochinche on the thirteenth floor turns
   neither to Henry's uninterrupted heroin business
   nor to the latest Twitter post from the Poetry Foundation.
Ever tried distilling last night's glocks and train screeches
   into a Petrarchan sonnet? Ever rhymed about rhyming?
   Ever made up the memories to fit the proper décima pattern?

   You do it every day,
this poeting between footsteps to the train, lovemaking on Sunday
because it's on your calendar, part-time prophecies
of Lower East Side minarets, and moving all her shit, again,
because you love her without needing to say it or write it down.

March 10, 1997

I don't know who
Pentecostals can't listen to
My high school is stung with
something I pretend to understand
for the sake of attaching myself to
the Walkmans that crawl
from the JanSports and suddenly
I am aware of how words
become notorious
  just died.

Biggie Smalls is
rap music
an excitable grief

some news
out

the Bible
something holy

Learning to Dance: The Rebellion
after Joe Arroyo's song "La Rebelión"

quiero contarle un pedacito—
            de la historia negra
de la historia nuestra—y dice así

(pom   pom pom)

los años the years carried my bones
            spun my hand, held my hair, & my aching
hips   flew between us & the song   lifted my skirt
            a flame tree   fluttering   against my cheek
& your lips   my legs a rebellion   *una rebelión*
            (pom)
                        (pom)
                                    (pom)
you lead the march across
            this wooden floor a tyranny of steps
syncopated rhythm   chained to   a matrimony of joy
            we find the freedom   this song is not
about   *esclavitud perpetua*
            (pom)
                        (pom)
                                    (pom)
I remember   a memory   my bisabuela may have had
            pink sunrise   behind a portrait of palmas
sucking sugar cane   sangre de cristo in my hair las amapolas
            gathered red   in the folds of my dress   I'd sing
esclava de un Español   el me daba muy mal trato
            (pom)
                        (pom)
                                    (pom)
across my face   black welts purplebruised beatings
            swell in my muscles   kissing dirt   lips burst open
like poppies   la tierra tastes bitter   passion fruit falling
& rotting   on knees I remember   a trumpet

tantrum pleading *salome, salome*
    (pom)
        (pom)
            (pom)
water   the ache & an ocean breaks   my tears
    while we dance   our skin slips sweat   & surrenders
luminous   our bodies bend beyond breaking
    my foot follows yours   free   from slavery
to salsa from captive to canto   from silence
to song we rebel: *hoy se escucha en la verja*
    (pom)
        (pom)
            (pom)
                we rebel: *no le pegue a mi negra*

Dancing in Buses

Pretend a boom box
blasts over your shoulder. Raise
your hands in the air. Twist them
as if picking limes. Look
to the right as if crossing
streets. Look to the left,
slowly as if balancing orange
baskets. Bend as if picking
cotton. Do the rump. Straighten
up as if dropping firewood. Rake,
do the rake. Sweep,
do the sweep. Do the pupusa-
clap—finger dough clumps. Clap.
Do the horchata-scoop—
your hand's a ladle, scoop.
Reach and scoop. Now,
duck. They're shooting. Duck
under the seat, and
don't breathe.

Hands behind your head.
Drop down.
Look at the ground.
Roll over.
Face the mouth of the barrel.
Do the protect-face-with-hand.
Don't scream.

Ode to Dipset

The group of young boys   huddled near
the emergency brake of the 1 train   carrying on

their sidekicks   Harlem's diplomats to the world:
Jim Juelz Cam   cocky rocking along with

the train   their voices
on the screeching tracks   skipping in certain sections

& the train car is packed   the men with briefcases &
the viejitas on their way home   cringe

but those boys   they grin& I too
quietly mouth the words.

It was on 79th street   when the old white lady
stood   seemingly innocuous

shuffled off through the open doors
but before the *ding*

& the reminder to *stay clear*   the old white lady
leaned her head back in   & loud enough

to disrupt the stifled air:

this is why we made you
sit on the back of the bus

                              & what none of us said: bitch   ain't you heard
                                          this here is a northbound train

                    & what none of us said: with yo' dusty-ass self   waiting
                                until the doors closing to say that shit

& what none of us said:

ayo   conductor   hold this train real quick

& what none of us said:

none of us had to say

because Dipset careened out of the phone speakers   all high horns & high-
    hats & high-ass
selves brash & bass   an anointment on our heads

spectacular yes! spectacular yes! spectacular yes!
one word to describe me   *spectacular yes!*

Eating Dinner Alone
at the 163rd Street Mall

As a kid I wanted to be
the first man on Mars,
pictured myself planting the stars

and stripes into the god of war's
face for all the universe to see,
becoming immortal.

I never imagined myself
at twenty-six grabbing a slapdash
dinner after class at the half-

abandoned 163rd street mall,
a break from bargain hunting because
it has both a Ross and a Marshalls

among the bootleg shops,
the vacant spaces, the *coming-
soon's* that will never be.

It's just me and the cashier
of *The Florribean,* the singular knight
in what passes for a food court,

and my order echoes through
the wide halls, the three-storied
ceiling, the way a death-

rower's last-meal request
must flood the stale air
of his concrete cell. I pay

in change and take my styrofoam
container of mismatched
island food to a table surrounded

98   by kiddie rides hungry for coins—
      a killer whale, sad as the real thing
      wasting away at SeaWorld,

      and beyond it a gleaming white
      rocketship with a glowing top
      and a strange, futuristic voice

      calling out to me, saying *please
      insert coin, please insert coin,*
      and for a moment I smile,

      consider cramming my adult body
      into that tiny command center,
      knees to chest, elbows tucked,

      let the rocking seize my imagination
      into ascent, up through the Earth's
      atmosphere until the sunlight

      falls away and all that's left
      is the naked sphere surrounded
      by the blackness of space.

      But the machine's constant
      plea reminds me that I'm doomed
      to be earthbound,

      star-crossed, having spent
      my last quarters on this cold
      jerk chicken, rice, and beans.

Jailhouse Library

They gave the homie
seven years when the dogs sniffed
a trunk full of
A People's History of the United States.
Battering rams crash the neighbor's
doorframe and they rush
the basement, confiscating pounds
of *A Light in the Attic.*
Automatic stop-and-frisk,
strange hands in the most intimate
parts of a shaking body, and maybe
a club to the mouth for anyone
who dares to openly carry
The Fire Next Time.
Police in riot gear hold
hands with legislators and clergymen
as if they're about to sing "We Shall Overcome,"
filling a pool with spit from their venomous
yelling and sweat from fear of
"pre-convicted" felons they cuffed
to the bottom of the pool.
They watch us *Drown.*

Making Love to Captain America

Sometimes I want to punch you in your perfect little teeth.
—Tony Stark

Could any human be more perfect?
He's all the pretty whiteness I was taught to want to
be or to have or to seduce maybe
with my Taíno-African tainafrican roots, my dusting of Europa
found in the D codon of my DNA somewhere near
the kink of my hair & the size of my breasts—

I am not sure how I love him more:
with his uniform off or on,
with the shield in front of him to ward off the enemy
or with his shield behind his back,
his arms left open for an embrace

He's always right, even when he's wrong, even when
he doesn't know the difference between the mouth open
for exit, or for entry

I want to make love to him

be wrapped up in all the stars & stripes of his conviction
I want to point out to him that the enemy is not always out there
Sometimes your enemy is your neighbor
Sometimes your enemy is some kid from Queens with daddy issues
Sometimes your enemy runs for president on your soil & calls you a thief
a rapist, a criminal, a choke in America's throat
Sometimes the enemy is forgetting that Cap & I can never see eye to eye
because he's been on ice so long he doesn't know

that America has become a dirty word that I only still use out of habit
That the habit is a secret thing I don't mention like my deep desire
for white boys & my constant need to break my body against them

Evolution has been unkind, Cap

Did you learn anything while you were cold?
Say yes & maybe there's hope for us all
Maybe we should all be put on ice too

Or maybe we should just let you loose
Will you destroy my enemies as easily as you do your own?
I don't want to know

The fantasy of you is so sweet
Let me stay sleeping

let me stay dreaming
& when I wake let me roll over
& see your face, pretty white boy
with pretty teeth, if I punch you
I am the only one that bleeds—

ode to new money

Jeremy says he want
that *shmoney*,
the kind of language
unwilling to count on itself.
I witness and am witnessed.
The *shh* of poverty
sinks my lips
into my father's
shoulders, the kind you engineer
a runaway from.
I always condemn
and yet stay.
A legacy I *whisper*
in the Bronx,
contain my throat within
Jeremy's bolted forearm.
I am my brother's
chokehold. I want
to break him—for all he knows
I cannot conceive.
Even he does not talk
the way my poems need him to.
Upstate, the leaves are the only brown
among the deer and *foliage*,
see, *see there*, I know the word
for money but not its origin.
In ninth grade I pronounced
the word wrong, not *the word*,
it's temperament, and the air shifts
the poverty in the train car
toward me. I am *never* the ghetto
I am the memory which deceives
its repetition. Jeremy knows this.
He has my father's eyes; I use
them to seal his tongue away.
This hunger for properness

has me renaming myself.
I am the deer no one resents
until it leaves the forest
and it's divine architecture—
how all green has a gate choking it.
I sell you this again and again,
I am the one
who gnaws on the diamonds
in the arches, who vomits
at company, but comes back
to turn my teeth to knives
as he did,
but my shoulders
they are so soft
and weighted
by nothing.

More Than One but Less Than Any
with lines from Kanye West

1.
There is a version of the story where you deserve to be forgiven.

2.
There are more where you are not.

3.
Everyone knows
I'm a motherfucking monster

4.
You, a Brown man, drive your child to school. A white teacher leans over you to
    speak to your child (almost white):
"Tell this to your father":
you can no longer remember how you got here—
this car, this street, this teacher leaning over you to speak with your child
    (white).
You are not forgiven for what happens next.

3.
The first time you hear someone read your name (not white) or
repeat it back to you without first pausing, deciding it

sounds different. But
you are too far (American) to ever
ever, ever.

2.
Your child (girl) sits by herself in the waiting room while you experience
dilation and something else.

The worst part, you'll tell her, is
they will all know what happened.
These people talk.

You (white) are
forgiven (it's not your fault), but that
is not the worst part, not ever.

1.
When you look at other people all you see is
worse versions of yourself.

Broken Sestina as Soundscape

How the room never danced because Pa never played
Juan Gabriel or other Mexican vocalists
in our house growing up. After crossing the border,
he must've ditched a suitcase of himself at US Customs.
Or maybe he never brought that suitcase. Maybe he wasn't mixed
about moving his kids to a middle-class neighborhood—

instead assimilating himself to cul-de-sac neighbors
so we could run outside with footballs and play
like all-Americans. In elementary school, I mixed up
my place, sat next to Danny and Michael until my voice
forgot its music. I became accustomed
to whiteness, neglected our border's

motherhood. I used to doodle in English, on the borders
of my notebook, before I visited Pa's childhood
home in Xalapa, before I knew how to trust the custom
of folding tortillas into each bite. Still, I never heard Pa play
Spanish music, would never catch him wandering the vocals
of a Vincente Fernandez solo. He never mixed

his past with our pleasures, preferred the mixture
of elegance and fine dining in flashy downtowns. He bordered
on being whitewashed, dreamed he'd be seen by the locals
who owned town homes all around us. He loved our neighborhood,
never wanted me to leave, was probably scared I'd play
around and discover earthquakes. I did. Customized

myself by learning how to change into costumes
when needed by blasting hip-hop. I have mixed
feelings about not knowing Pedro Infane's lyrics, about playing
more Tupac than mariachis. I've become a borderland
of tongues, a mezcla of eyes. I've navigated unknown neighborhoods
around Mexico and follow the rhythm of an inner voice

telling me to fly far away, because most days I feel voiceless
and misguided, accustomed
to breakages. But I've learned to break neighborhoods
open and let oceans swim inside me, a mixtape
of blood and knuckles swelling unbordered
soundscapes, something new in my stereo always playing.

Ode to Tego Calderón
(or The Day *El abayarde* Dropped Was Maelo's Resurrection)

it isn't the salsa-backed intro
on the cover, mirror held up
nariz into boca, drip molasses
to el sonero mayor, sonero-
no bomba interludes
maelo owned in villa palmeras
the *ecuajey* you sing like him
tú eres guasa guasa we
los prietos, los niches
played back in reverse
taking place on stage
negra son un desfile
se alegra

horns heralding his salsa vieja
esto fue lo que trajo el barco
to bemba. voz is drenched in it
improv mutates over breakbeat
bring us back to santurce
the "witinila" sample
your nod to loíza and
direct to puerto rico
styled yourself abayarde
hand pushing out of casket
singing one more time
de melaza en flor que cuando
de su negrura todo

the fro you sport
the way you dip
make your vocal copy
and dembow ricochet
rumbones de esquina
in "salte del medio"
los difuntos and the cry
a los afroboricuas, los negros
and maelo's entierro
nazareno clutching mic
las caras lindas de mi gente
pasa frente a mí
el corazón

Poem Ending and Beginning on Lines by Larry Levis

Because you haven't praised anything in months,
and because iron, because two ten-pound plates—
when pressed to six wheels and late sets—are enough
to drive better men to dust, and because the young bucks
curling near the mirror have paused their pretty work
to watch your old ass snatch from the bench's
buckling uprights all three hundred and thirty-five
goddam pounds, you summon the saint of iron,
the blacksmith in palm skirt fisting his machetes,
to give you just a little bit of what you need to bring it
down, to bang it up, just once. Just this once.
—*Ago, Baba Mi. Ogun Owanile O, Ogun, Cobu Cobu.*

Of course, the young bucks chuckle at this ooga-booga
babble, this strange ritual gibberish of an old-timer,
obviously—in the parlance of the place—dead set
to fuck his self up. But you break the weight, you do.
And the room falls quiet but for the quiver and clang
of iron on iron, the few slim seconds it takes to turn
back time. Lift off, and you're a young man in an old city.
No beard, no gray. Lift again, and Parliament is pulsing
from a ghetto blaster perched on a pair of milk crates
in a neighbor's yellow yard, your sixteen-year-old self
is writhing under another bar, what feels like two tons
crushing you dead, and Robert Caldwell's glaring
from behind the bench, yelling for you to drive it all up.

Robert Caldwell, barrel-chested, chiseled, and damn
near three hundred pounds, who pushed a pallet jack
for twelve-hour shifts, after twenty-something years
stretched across San Quentin, Soledad, and Folsom;
Robert Caldwell, the triple OG, who once threatened
his boss with a box cutter for wolfing loud, or holding
eye contact a little too long, has for reasons unknown

chosen you for his pet project, promising to forge you
into something unbreakable. Said by summer's end,
you, too, will have grown men flinching when you flex,
and the women—*oh, the women*—will make disappear
all the deep, deep ache a man inflicts on himself. Or,
rather, all the pain Robert Caldwell will inflict on you.
For make no mistake, this will be a summer that hurts.

Deadlifts, box squats, power cleans, and curls.
The eggs yolks nasty, the slither down your throat.
Drop sets, pyramids, twenty-ones, and cheats. The day
you learned how Robert Caldwell found his father
dead. Days dead the day before, a stolen Desert Eagle
spent and sprawled near what once was a face.
Robert Caldwell drops this on you hard between sets,
but doesn't pause to break down sobbing. *Push, nigga.
Push*, says Robert Caldwell. *Pain is weakness leaving.*
Push, nigga. Push. Become something unbreakable.
Robert Caldwell doesn't break or take a day to mourn,
or ring your phone late night to chat about regret,
or counsel you to love better than you've been.
He does what any good ironworker does. He works.

And he works you. All summer long. Sets and reps
and pressure and flame and all the requisite ache.
You don't break, exactly, but come close to buckling.
That summer, and summers since. So much burn,
so much weight. So much. You'll leave three women,
the rest will leave you first. You'll bury your own father,
lose four friends to gunfire, one to a jailhouse noose.
Your hands will shame you often. But first, this.
OG Robert Caldwell, his jigs, blocks, and hammer.
OG Robert Caldwell, backlit by the sun. *Ogun
Owanile O, Ogun Cobu Cobu.* How beautiful this man,
his trust in iron, what it gives us, what it takes.
What it gives again. He yells for you to push, you push.

Robert Caldwell, you think, would have loved this
beat-down Brooklyn hole-in-the-wall, its ripped leather
seat-backs, all its stale air. He'd have loved the rusty
dumbbells, the dirt-caked mirror, the young bucks

circling you now, watching and waiting. You stare hard
into that mirror, into your beard and gray. Crow's feet
and furrows. Thirty-something summers and you've become
the triple OG. Every ache you've earned tells you so.
The young bucks clock you as you lay back on the bench,
your hands chalked and finding their grip. *Weight,*
you think, *they don't have a clue.* You break the bar
from its rack, feel it all bearing down. The quiver and heft,
the sudden, overcast quiet of the past tense.

Nunca seré fina

Nunca seré fina pero tampoco soy sencilla
bailando reguetón desde niña
liberación en las marquesinas

I'm a Libra
catch me en la esquina
spreading flyers, handing out ideas
Dudes tryna look back at it like I'm Trina
Lip gloss popping, call me Lil' Dita
La revolución va tai encendía
Fuego en la cintura y fuego a la oligarquía
Soy puta pero picky, call me fresita
Sepo más rico que el postre de su marida
Los pongo en cuclilla a comer de gratis, así les llenó la barriga
now you can call me Mother Teresa

But for real tho let me reintroduce myself
Yo soy Amanda Alcántara con acento en la A
La palabrista
La que se hacía llamar dique Radical Latina
La que confunden de niña teniendo de reina la pinta
La que se inventa frases porque vive entre dos lenguas y cinco vidas
Hija, hermana, puta, santa, y amiga
Y bésame la mano
que también soy tu madrina
La que se ve buena aunque no corre ni una milla
That bitch you hate cuz you assumed she's problematic but she's still about
    freedom
Más que Frida, yo soy la de artes de autocrítica
Tú te crees woke pero sigues a las mases, yo sigo a la vida
I'm the spirit to your Sprite
The electricity pa' tus pilas
The one that hits you a escondidas
Y cuando se va, se siente
Emotional diva
Unconventional liricista

Underestimated leader
Watching me walk away
es un privilegio para tus ojos
y un deseo pa tu boquita
Me prefieren muerta porque mi boca es muy grande para sus ideas vendidas
Pero esta rosa no se marchita
Call me Margarita
Y te lo repito por si se te olvida
Nunca seré fina pero tampoco soy sencilla

Round Two: Saving Nations

APOLLO: Damn man! What the hell you doin'? This man will knock
you on your ass! You thought I was tough? This chump will kill yah.
Come on! What's the matter with you?

ROCKY: Tomorrow. Let's do it tomorrow.
—Rocky III

THERE IS NO TOMORROW

Josefo's college roommate once believed it
necessary to take over Wheeler Hall at Berkeley,
chain the doors, and hold off the police for many
days. There are many well-recorded facts that could
have motivated such an action. When asked to
explain himself, his roommate recited this Mario
Savio line from memory:

There comes a time when the operation of the
machine becomes so odious, makes you so sick at
heart, that you can't take part, you can't even
passively take part and you've got to put your
bodies upon the gears and upon the wheels, upon
all the apparatus, and you've got to make it stop.

Ishmael Armendariz, known to his Grandmother
and only his Grandmother as *Ismael*, explained the
need for direct action in this manner. Commenting
further, Ish went on to recall Tupac's famous poetic
metaphor of the rose that grew from concrete.
Ishmael said that we should encourage and foster
the growth of these roses, yes, but that this was not
enough. The problem lies not with the roses, no; the
problem is one of concrete. Ishmael said:

We roses have to do more than show off our pretty
petals. We roses must grow hands and feet. We roses
must remove the concrete, man, or none of this shit is

THERE IS NO TOMORROW

(Fool, dontchuknow
revolution is just romance?)
Martín Espada wrote something
about a lover's hands
Circling Grasping Clasping
(Huggin 'n' Shit) Tellin' Me
You Know Nothing of Love.
I asked instead for a bus pass
like a smartass on his way to mass—
not a donkey, but the thing we carry behind us.

>   *Dear Professor Marcial Gonzalez,*
>
>   *I hate to be the one to deliver this message
>   but the poet known as Luis Omar Salinas
>   also known as: The Crazy Gypsy
>   also known as: Salinas
>   also known as: The Aztec Angel
>   also known as: Omar*
>
>   *died while performing the Salinas Shuffle.
>   He will not be available for a reading now or
>   in the future.*
>
>   *Javier and I wanted to buy a photo
>   of him and Jose Montoya,
>   the grandfather of us all,
>   but we couldn't afford
>   the $100 price tag.   Oh yeah
>   I'm still wrestling with your section on
>   the Parataxis-Hypotaxis Antinomy
>   Honestly   parts of it are still too much
>   for a dirty-faced mocoso like me but
>   something about it makes a lotta sense.*
>
>   *Abrazo,
>   JR*

Meanwhile
back at the ranch:

Billie Dee sellin' malt liquor,
the Beave huffin',
through a Che T-shirt,
Mexicanitos multiply
in third-grade classrooms,
& Freddy Soto's still dead.
   Regardless,

Richmond Amtrak,
thinking on Calwa,
Grandma's bobby pins,
hoodied passengers,
Rockyesque docks,
Barbed-wire grays,
Endor Walkers,*

   See the sea

          needs protection
          from the nakedness
          of your brown toes,

itchy chin hair,
bald head—no beanie,
words like Justice
& Stylistic in all of it.
Gimme a bigote

---

* CORRECTION: Recently Josefo was made aware of a gross error in his referencing. While reading an early draft of this poem at their grandmother's house, his cousin, a superior *Star Wars* fan, pointed out that the Walkers most resembling the Oakland cranes were never on Endor. In fact, the walkers that appear on the forest moon in *Return of the Jedi* were much smaller. Josefo hoped to reference the All Terrain Armored Transport (AT-AT) Walkers, also known as the Imperial Walkers, famed for their contribution to the Rebel Alliance's defeat at the Battle of Hoth during the Galactic Civil War.

George Lucas says he did not model their design after the dock cranes set about the Oakland coastline, but George Lucas is full of shit. Everyone knows this. The author thanks Gabriel Pacheco for this correction.

for all seasons
like Coppolla,
Samuel Beam,
Furious Styles,
Fidel Castro,
Monk &
Common Sense

Muse Found in a Colonized Body

Outside the bodega it is spring
a sixty-degree evening & the men
are playing dominoes. Their
granddaughters with pigtails
& pink bomber jackets & matching
leggings are hopscotching, I take
a turn before going inside—

On the line I hold onto a bag of
perejil, una yautia, dos yucas,
y un carton de huevos. Tonight
dinner is a Taíno feast—& this
is where my mind has wandered
when the white woman slides in
front of me. She slams her Diet Coke,

bag of butter lettuce, box of Rice-
a-Roni, & a can of tuna on the
counter. El bodegero looks in
my direction; he knows I carry
inside me the kind of ancestors
that would cut a bitch, but I say
nothing. The air that comes through

the door is so soft like a lover's
sweet hands & I am feeling generous.

You should carry organic eggs, then
I don't have to go to the supermarket
so out of my way. The bodegero asks:
Are you going to buy all my organic

foods if I order them? She responds:
Yes, me & all my friends. I stop
paying attention; behind the glass
counter are three Dominican

newspapers on display. One
of the captions stops me—

Exclusivo, Quién Era Cristóbal Colón?

In an instant I am giggling
uncontrollably. I have no idea
who he was, but I know at the very
least he was the kind of human
that landed in a place some called
paradise & instead of enjoying the view

he asked for organic eggs & cut the line—

In the Reunion of All My Selves

the one still in Brazil does all the cooking,
has yellow turmeric stains under her nails.
The one still in church insists we pray

before we eat, dares someone to say no,
sits beside the one with tattoos
and listens to stories she deems mistakes.

One of us has forgotten
Portuguese but uses Spanish to get by.
One says science and magic are the same,

hands out pamphlets for the new planet
she is building, says everyone would be welcome.
One sends a letter in her stead. She hasn't left home

in decades, couldn't work up the nerve
to make this exception. She sends her regards.
Over a meal of *molho de frango* spread over white rice,

the women who are me do not ask each other questions.
They are afraid. Instead, they complain about time,
never admitting the longing to switch lives,

and decide to go back to what they know, even if it's all fire.
Even if all they know is burning.
But outside, before goodbyes, the one who's a witch

creates a bonfire, insists they all stand in a circle,
and as the one who's a singer sings
their favorite song, their held hands become

more water than flesh,
bodies more dust than solid,
and in their swaying, the women slip

into oneness,
like a foot slides into an old shoe,
and for a moment, all my selves feel whole.

Becoming a "City-Sent"

When Mexican parents
come to America
they refuse to change their tradicion
the way they refuse to
buy a new pair of chanclas

A mother who just received
documentos to be in this country
attempts to string her first
gringa words together
I am a City-Sent

She claims
Yo se who es el
primer presidente
Jorge Washington
It was the only answer she
truly knew
or believed

Puras mentiras that come
out of the gueros mouths
The doctor es
mentiroso
El banco Chase es
mentiroso
The teacher es
mentiroso
Until the truth comes
out
in a student
parent-teacher conference
Now you are the mentiroso

Mama didn't make it to *el trabajo*
All the hard work

that could've been
put into her chancla
is gyrating toward your head
Beat the grading scale
out of me
in order to beat
the honor roll into me

A small smack in the end
para que me porte bien
in reality just for
the sake of being the son
of a Mexican mom
because now she is a City-Sent

does not have to be paid
less than she deserves
And I'm a mentiroso now
don't have to be smacked
less than I deserve
a tradition we
are selfish with
The gringos will
never taste the
hard work edges
of my mother's chancla
Never taste the
agua bendita when my
behavior was because of a demonio
Gracias
por sacarme
The fantasma of Jorge Washington
por re partir-
me la madre
when I didn't understand
cuanto
te partias
la tu ya

Phone Call: A Shitty Play in One Act

[it starts as a phone call in a classroom in El Paso]

DANIA (my sister): hey fool, call mom right now!
the fuckin' migra got Gove!

JESUS (me): "migra,"
USCIS, ICE now, CBP always
beast howling thirsty outside our doors,
unless of course, you are what you might be—
a citizen.
the professor in front of the classroom
is explaining the importance of august wilson's "pittsburgh cycle" on american
    theatre,
how some bodies are made visible,
how some bodies disappear.
i can't hear him clearly.
on the other end of the phone is my thirtheen-year-old sister
and the whole world cracked open.

i wasn't there when the ICE agents raided my brother's work.
i only saw the news stories,
and what hurt most immediately was thinking about him on the ground,
about his hands behind his head.
what hurt most was thinking about the chaos—
the running through the rocks and the dust and cement.
twenty-eight men,
one of them my brother, [GOVELIN ARREOLA MORALES],
and if i write his name down—right here—spell it
right in all this English,
[GOVELIN ARREOLA MORALES]
and if someone reads this [GOVELIN ARREOLA MORALES],
isn't he documented? aren't these his papers?
what hurt most of all
was watching my mother receive a call from him,
from inside that detention center,

the precise moment she heard his voice crack,
this man made from stone—and she says

ROSA (my mother): te quiero, mijo.

*[and what hurt most was the way the government sopped up the mess they made
with paper, and none of the characters exit, and the lost brother is always off-stage, a
voice somewhere]*

end of play.

When Collin Chanted "Build the Wall"

at me, the teacher didn't say anything,
and the rio grande started
to drown my father again.
i had to drag my dad out
in the middle of the classroom
and swallow him.

Papi, Papá

I catch my head again.
I expect to see my father
entering a room. I catch
my head starting to turn

and I'm on the disappearing end
of an island, thinking of
the girl from El Salvador
whose sentences

are polite in a recording
from migrant detention.

They identify countries
of origin, not names. A crying
boy from Guatemala

says *Papi, Papi, Papá.* Dad, Daddy,
Father, I miss you. Please walk

through the door again.
Please inhabit your body.

Does he construct
a memory or a daydream
where his father, wearing the last

outfit he was seen in, enters
from the other side of a cage?

When I try to rebuild my father
it's his hair first, his shoulders, scenarios
of posture. I couldn't see

the last thing he wore. I had
the opportunity,

A child doesn't understand
separation. Absence is

a game: disappearance,
reappearance, a face
behind hands. I was there

the morning my father
crossed an undeniable border
and a boy is at the border now.

He catches his head
turning, looking

to the door and back, Papi,
Papá, and the country beyond

the facility is desert and
wire and everything, everything

in this wide cold
place is a pale-yellow polo,
tucked in at the waist.
A shirt his father wore.

The Bridge Is Out

but it won't stop us, amigax—
we underwater walk. A is but a myth,
an attempt to keep us from discovery.
You'll drown, men heckle, but as our hermanx knew,
there's a world beyond

their reach. After all, our days are not
meant to be halcyon and no language conventions
can hold them. We drive away from wreckage,
legs up on the dashboard, can't no one tell us nothing.

Quiero escuchar. Quiero cantar.

No dungeon, no dragon, no such thing as a linguistic
        misstep.
        We drop verbs, drop whole goddamn sentences, & we're prepared to
pay for it.
        I'm coming straight animal, so meet me there, sabes?
        There are movements beyond academia, beyond roads, beyond
        what our Pops told us. *Dime*, is there a stop along the way?

No.

Every time Caesar calls, we shoot Patrón.

Our Love on the Other Side of This Border

Maybe, I would have seen you trip
over the steps in the patio between
classes, or we would have met on the
soccer field covered in mud, and you
would have asked my name, that crooked
smile spreading from your eyes to your
mouth. Maybe I would have laughed.
Maybe, we would have had a nieve in the
plaza, and you would have held my hand
after folklórico or at a fandango where I
was learning to dance faster than my
adrenaline. Maybe, you would have given
me a bouquet of mango con chile y limón,
or elote con queso and we'd count all the
ways cuetes go off in this pueblo, and would
walk the feria at night wrapped up in blankets
drinking atole. Maybe, we would have fought
over the meaning of God, maybe, that danzón
after drinking the toritos would have made me
cry. Maybe, I would have broken your heart over
a plate of tamales and ponche or, maybe you
would have cut me off with a joke. But maybe
this land would have been large enough for our
hearts to grow, the sun would feel different on
our skin and the mercados with the viejitas
would give a calmer pace to our lives. Maybe, our
cuts would be different here, with enough
medicina to move through saltwater. Maybe, our
roots would allow our bones to be enough.

The Language in Question

The language in question is criminal // like a shark it ate a license plate // and it ate the shark // well the fins it poached anyway // it gorges like a gorge // the river flowing like a scarf someone kept pulling // it ate away the deposits of clay // like a sinkhole the language in question // ate a chateau and the family inside // it pickpockets the stranger with gusto // it barters with bards // pays in counterfeit // money is no object // the tongue desires // the language acquires // the language in question likes conquest // moves west because it hungers like locust // like the larvae of the caddisfly // this tongue makes a shell of what it pilfered // it's the apex predator in the food pyramid // it ransacked the pyramids // tours the spoils of theft to the country of origin // but only on loan // a paper wasp that makes its home from what it chewed and spat back out of your own // and it stings you if you get too close // too close // stung // I told you the language in question is the S-shaped tongue of the anteater // the so-called worm tongue // it warms itself at the fire it made from other people's scrolls // codices // tomes // it entombs and embalms and lights bombs // the language in question thinks it's Billy the Kid // the language in question is shooting up the saloon // the language in question is shooting up meth // dope // coke // whatever's on hand is the drug of choice // the language in question is corrupt // it's poison and salve // savage and sage // it's honeysuckle and bitter oleander // only a lawyer could make sense of it // and sell it to the highest bidder// like a snake that ate a parrot whole // spits out the bright feathers // without a bird to hold them together // that's what it's like when the accent doesn't even come close // the language gets twisted // the tongue gets tired // I'd bet it's kinky and likes to be tied // likes every bit of itself bit // this tongue bids adieu // holed in the mouth // ah-dee-ose // ah-mee-goes

English

It made
    its home   hovering

           around my body
        the first four years of my life
      Sometimes, it tired
             and rested
    in my shadow
             trailed slimy red and sticky but
   always   waited
     knew my hatred would pass
     that I'd find my way to its lap
                       soon
     I'd rest my head on its shoulder
   curl up against fragmented bone
      and let it dig its hands around my spine

    English was patient   because it knew
   it would win   in this country
           I wouldn't
be able to resist much longer

               Sometimes I can still hear
               English's cackling
               when at four years old
               I proclaimed:
                     ¡No me hable así!
     ¡Yo no hablo ingles y nunca lo hablaré!

   Weeks later   in kindergarten
   I let English reign over
              my body
   let myself soak   in its liquid power

dizzied myself in this winding river made its waters the language I tell stories in
    built a home in its classes   declared a major in its body

chased it up the Thames   to the world's oldest English-speaking university
        tossed away Spanish   reserved it for Saturdays   sometimes
 or visits to grandma's
and even now   the only Spanish that lives in this poem is faint
memory   the
words of a younger   braver   self

           and now I'm afraid
           'cause I bet English is sitting
           somewhere in this room
                clutching its stomach
           rolling over in laughter
                at how I typed these words
                sometimes first in Spanish
                then backspaced my return to English.

           English laughs

           and laughs

           and laughs.

Amaizeing Grace

Amazing Grace, how sweet the sound,
That saved a wretch like me.
I once was lost but now am found,
Was blind, but now I see.

Amaze A Maze A maze a maze a Maze a Maize a maize maíz maíz amazing
   AMazeIngles amazing Maíz amazing grace gracias maíz Mazing mazes
   amaizing grace mas maíz, gracias

Si! pote   nte   soy porque siempre como maiz
because mira que this life is a mazeing for me, y
mi lengua harbors trap doors, y
mi garganta was built with a secret passageway (no me recuerdo donde, but it is
   somewhere), y
te lo digo de experiencia, it's too dangerous to walk alone, vos
(yet too narrow para traer toda la mara, bicho!)
Puro maze,
it's by design homie: no way out (carajo. . . e que me olvido the way in too)
Pero maze can be beautiful, celebramos this identity que es
Puro maize, harvested like a cornfield, que no?
We are men of maize, ¡they said!   So you see homie es nuestra onda
What's wrong with being "lost"?
Wanna be "found"? Remember the last time you were "discovered"?
No'hombre, primo, lose yourself rather.   emptiness is there to feed you.

                        To offset hunger is *rellenar*
                                  hinchar
                              pupushahua

Y mira, su mamá over there making pupusas
that's all you, bro
        puro technique, art, and physics all gyrating on your mamá's hands
                the kitchen has always been where our pantheon meets
            not even Martha Stewart could make them, tu sabes
only we know
you first gotta own these veins, chero. you gotta
                    become
                        the ma(í)ze.

Translation

My mother hangs up the phone
scrapes loose the tears
prepares to tell me
who is dying   this time

I speak no Spanish
My mother is the translator
of the dying
My family is always the dying
I say family despite the fact
I have attended none of their funerals

My abuelita was a ricocheting ghost
She died once   and I forgot
an entire language

Okay   I didn't forget
it just became inconvenient to remember
Who wants a language for the living anyway?

An inventory of my tongue
yields nothing
that looks like my mother
The resemblance stops at the mouth

She is fluent in a language
I am only ever ugly in
She falls asleep in front of the TV
her show muted
I wonder if in her dreams
I can speak

Indubitable

Consider approach: will remainder be frozen into stylish unknown revealed to chosen few once party reaches peak lit, nobody wants to hear fancy forms, yesterday's lean, unrealistic schemes although we all like to waste today in funniest way possible, to forget freedom, further from satisfaction than next flame, fam, don't fight how much you want to light up the sky, night heals then morning reminder of past damage unaccounted then released contract, your hieroglyphic cryptocurrency back on market, no speculation consistent investment, ordinary operation, go 'head, run, under sun, can't hide from no one, confident blood etch rigid resolution; without faith within, no ears shall listen, ready to leave before redemption arrived can't decide to begin as game no longer played, what else is available besides standby reservoir of ancestral rage that sounds like mother cursing out father for all failed to fix, doors closed somehow unlocked, stood on gray, square, cinder block, holding ten-pound brown dumbbell eating neon-orange cheez doodles under red bulb, white light, police blew past, last allowed in silent romance, that replays lonely abandonment, comedic snores before brief words from overseeing sponsor, right back to this enthusiastic obtuse angle crunching ruins *presta'o* for inebriated amusement enlightened elevation ascending with flutter of majestic ritual, your strained laughter is most beautiful miracle can master, then let that hog cackle faster when next joke dangling like shorty with the face, who got feet I got socks, flabbergasted flummoxed blubbering walrus, thirsty tortoise, angry hyena panting munchiest breath, wistful coqui hoping for more love, but glassy page like empty pond, might be all the amor you get.

Factory Outlet

This hole's got
a hold on
me and a hole's
only hope is
to grow. Brushed
heather, herring-
bone twill, Japanese
chambray—no,
what are the words
for these feelings?
Look in the
window at all of
these winners!
These mirrors
aren't what
we think they
are, neither are
we. Subjects
and objects,
the need to re-
predicate. To be
an American's
to be un-
American
when Americans'
only kin-
ship is
with shit.
"Let's go"
as in let
us let us
let us let
us go

Blood

There was blood evidence, and still
the culprit got away. There was surveillance
footage, a positive ID. There was a smoking
revolver. We know who did it. There was blood
on his shoes. There were fingerprints
on the trigger. There were eyewitnesses.
There were multiple videos. There was power
of the press. Attorneys were involved. It was
a done deal, an open and shut case. It
was justice or bust. The blood was on
the wall, a message was written in the empty
street. There were no sidewalks. There
was no way to abide. It was an abomination,
an outrage. The people were outraged. This is
not the way lives are supposed to be. This is
a free world, a free country, a free one walking,
a free America. Free America. Free all
who walk therein. No man is created
unequal. We are all women on the face
of the earth. We walk in beauty in the shadow
of the police. All hail the barrage of gunfire
upon us. All notice and hail, the hail of blood
this time.

Advice to a Migrant Collecting
Dead Things Ever Since
He Learned the Length of Walking

Leave them. Only
heavy clothing
        in a knapsack.
Don't talk
    or make a sound. We
        don't want anyone
to hear our lips utter
    God be wicked or God be askew
        with you. From now on
all roots & runners
    will contain a silence
        you've never known,
a life grown all of its
    own. Don't look back
        to the slightest point
of light. Not much
    can be done until
        we get out. Leave it.
The smallest
    possibility to pull
        your country.
Leave it. It's pitch
    December, it's abridged
        tremor, saying
here's your country
    broken by rain, here's
        how puddles
carve a pothole
    out of your head, how
        night dented
buckles over
    the highway, abandoned

by some wrecked
lanterns, dim single-bulb houses
    gone completely quiet
saying enough,
enough of you.

Leaked Audio from a Detention Center

On June 2018, leaked audio from inside a US Customs and Border Protection Detention Facility captured undocumented children crying. An anonymous source handed the recorded audio to civil rights attorney Jennifer Harbury and also gave it to ProPublica for release.

hear how the children   eat their tears

how the rain   in their throats   demands to be a river

yet their palms be: drought   dirt grave   dead fish

quiet rock   anchor rust   but know this:

grief can be   a kind of music   that knows how to rise

    like the sea

Regeneration Spell for the Grieving Soul: Ingredients and Tools w/ Instructions

// *cinnamon* (good for cuts)

// *savila,* like that resilient aloe vera my sister gave me
when we worked at that racist stockyard job
—these plants don't die from malas vibras,
not even when those white men
—smelling like car fuel and murder—
yelled at us for existing

// that *avocado mascara* from the Mexican grocery
store (keep those eyes sharp & lined for protection)

// *one Bodak Yellow candle that becomes gold; pyrite*

elements: (gather one of each to represent the elements)

// *air: feather; cigarette (faros); las carcajadas of my dead tías*
who drank mezcal & fucked different men. the ones who turned into owls

// *water: the seafoam walls of my grandmother's home*
in Guadalajara; the holy water your mother gives you in recycled
Bath and Body Works bottles with a Sharpie sign reading "Agua Bendita";
coin pearls

// *earth: acrylic nails; hands with Hot Cheeto dust; gold amulets from our parents;*
    my mother
gave me an esclava with my name on it and three kinds of gold; she tells me if i
    ever need to eat,
pawn it

// *fire: menstrual blood; blunts; poetry; faros*

// *salt;*

// *rosewater*

// *needle & thread*

mix all materials & drink

// *find a circular ruin*
// *fall asleep*
// *dream*

Mexican Remedies

When I tell my tías
that I have a stomachache
they cure me of empacho and
feed me olive oil with salt
and seltzer con limón.

When I tell my tías
that I have a cold
they make me caldo de pollo,
they put Vaporú on my chest
and even under my feet.

When I tell my tías
that I have a cough
they tell me to drink
a shot of tequila o aguardiante,
porque eso lo cura todo.

But when I tell my tías
that I am depressed or
have anxiety they tell
me to pray it away,
they tell me to just move on
with my life and not think about it.

There are no Mexican
remedies for that.

"You're Not Even Black," a White Man Tells Me Outside the Club

Picture an early hunter-gatherer, around five or six;
horizontal, calloused bare feet
pointed toward the moonlight, stiffening

like his heartbeat.
The tomatoes he'd spotted and eaten just a few of
before grabbing the rest to share

were actually horse nettles.
Picture being still so new to the solo forage,
never even considering it could be poison.

So innocent—sorry, scratch that.
A clear villain pacifies all harm.
Picture he was a foolish, lazy, grown man,

who hoarded food beneath fruitless briars.
As he draws still, the others grow faster:
freshly unburdened, and with new wisdom.

Seventh Grade, Discussing Halloween at the Cafeteria Table, Surrounded by the Homies

so then pepe asks about trick-or-treating & because
it's his first octubre in texas & not spent in zacatecas

it's later that school night when we peel out
the neighborhood & drive to the suburbs

& what we did for sweets back then was vocational
often a vacation,   seldom offered outside of season

riding backseat,   our old gray van a   spaceship   my dad
used to pilot everywhere,   asteroid belt

conducing—i mean conducting,   digo,   conduciendo
cero en conducta   duct
tape & desarm

adores inside the toolbox
rattling in the

back, until gas got to almost four dollars a gallon.
so now it stays parked in the driveway.

used to pick me up after band practice
                                            in the bucket.

once, i was one of the last ones waiting outside, rainy
day maybe, four other kids, fools,   goofball grinning

cheek to cheek   always,   like some joker cards
we took out the deck to play slapjack with.

& I must've been watching too much george lopez back then

dad   has a van like that.

like it was some kinda joke   what my dad   made his bread in.

& mr. jaime said at least you have a ride
home. and the engine runs. a worthy

chariot. i don't remember anyone laughing as i swung
open the door & hopped in the van,   but I remember cinco

corridos a las cinco   on the radio always,   cranking the knob on the a/c
like maybe this time it would cough up more than just dust

my dad driving beside me wearing the same mustache & hat,   gooseneck,
never crooked,   still eating from the same lunchbox since the eighties.

both of us swallowing silence.
but in outerspace we're howling

now & pepe is looking rather grim,
scythe & all,   a robe draped over him,   wearing

it like an extra shadow,   a dark cloud with some thunder
bolts,   holding onto a plastic pumpkin

he'd bought the day before at sam's club
where he went shopping with Doña Ortencia & it was dollars not pesos.

back in the van, we try to teach pepe how to say trick
or treat   but he keeps rolling his *r*'s and saying treat
so it sounds like eat but we just laugh and say fuck

it bro, you got it, it don't matter,   because it doesn't,   not really,   not to us,
    cuz   if we're cool
like that then we're cool & we're all kinds of hungry. now

we get to the row of houses with streetlights that never flicker & we hop
out the van ready to go out into the night & be ghostlike & ravenous,

chocolate m&m's & miniature bags of skittles on the mind as we float
across yards mowed every saturday morning & garage-sale weekend,

the soft sighs of grass perfectly cut reaching out to brush against our skin,

my mom & dad following behind from atop
of the elephant,   listening to brindis.

so we ring doorbells of houses where strangers live & they come outside like
     they've been
expecting us

so we haunt them, hood-
ed figures underneath their porch lights
several decades too soon,   apparitions,   three reapers,   masks bone-

white,   though underneath our skeleton
faces,   pepe suddenly betrays us,   speaks up &   punctuates

the air with language,   his accent
an accident   that had to happen

& maybe they hesitate because they think his mouth
says eat but its shape means devour,   means swallow   whole or
     be swallowed,   but he holds

out his purple pumpkin anyway   and smiles as he receives their meager
     blessing, a mini sneak—
snickers,   satisfied?,

we head back to the street,   the van,   &   the headlights, scooby
& the gang
or something   &   that

night

we never stop running to the next house

Tonight's Blackout

fault on transmission line   the grid dropped
and eventually outage   the deep sigh of dimming lights
all long-blink   for the outrage   of an endless forty-eight hours

got pressed   with flat lines   distressed temples
bent brows   based off the uncertainty
based off the constant jettison

the coconut gets more light than luis   and at dawn
i fell asleep at the gas station and i'm told there is   enough
but we stay waiting   this year has been unplugged respiration

i need breath   and un pastelón calientito
and representation in the senate   this is big stick mi pana   speak softly
save your voice   they take it   in rhythm   the way nurse treats pulse

Immigration Story

I was ten years old when I read about the boy
whose mother drowned in the ocean.

It was in the *Scholastic News*—
the aluminum boat leaving Cuba,

the shipwreck, the ten more dead with her,
the boy floating on an inner tube until rescued by fishermen.

His face was on the front page of the magazine
and I wanted to kiss his paper cheek. His name

is Elián and today he turns twenty-three.
My mother shows me a picture

of his mother. She is beautiful in the way
all mothers were in the 90s—

all bangs, high-waisted jersey shorts.
And I don't know what it is to lose a mother

yet. I won't see her scoop water from a sinking boat.
My mother came here

on a plane and I thank a god. A different
island, a different year, a baby girl,

not me, in her arms.
Elián went back to Cuba.

And I have never visited the island I'm from.
And I feel like a bitch.

Because all I did was read a story,
then retell it on this page.

In Response to People Trying to Rename the South Bronx "The Piano District"

Of course they only see
the white keys—not the dark
veins that feed the heart
and sing.

nimbus 1999

people, my people, I want to speak to my people
y cuando digo my people quiero decir Mi Pueblo

wherever my pueblo is wherever I'll find my people,   quiero
decir, dónde está mi gente está Mi Pueblo

give us the keys to a new city or we will imagine ourselves a new one,
make it seem like the wizarding

world   is parallel   to the real one,
except our Hogwarts is somewhere in Houston

and Diagon Alley is a flea market
Tía Pancha's off Telephone,   and saturdays

are when   horchata works
as a love potion, hand-holding, hibiscus

fake stereos, & fresh fruit, no Hedwig, or

phoenixes, but in the back somewhere
some roosters & highlighter canaries in cages, dried

chiles, light-up sneakers, and bowl cuts, no chocolate
frog leaps but Bulbasaur ivy whips if you level him.
semi-permanently   stuck in the 90s

my people
don't use floo powder but collect phone cards,

forget to call home so often   they   learn to call people
home.

¡Wepa!

My blood is so hot and wet right now. I know they want it.
                                                        —Morgan Parker

Why did I kill them? At the party I yelled *¡wepa!* & just before I closed my mouth a white woman grabbed my tongue & cut it out. The horn wailed; kept vigil for eight counts. She tied my tongue to a string & hung it around her neck. I lunged for her neck but just then a white man grabbed my hand for a dance. He was an aggressive lead, but I couldn't say *no*—my cheeks were filling with blood. If I messed the floor, the other dancers would've blamed me for ruining their night. He spun me.

Each spin was more aggressive than the last. Behind him at the door I saw the white woman & I tried to spot my tongue, but she'd acquired new tongues so I couldn't tell mine from the others. Each spin dizzied me & reminded me of what I'd lost. But I couldn't spill the blood, so I spotted using the bundle of tongues around her neck until I spun again & she was gone. I fell. The white man did not try to catch me & was angry that I'd ruined his dance.

I left the party to find someplace to spill all the blood until, gracias a Díos, I spotted a Latino. I wanted to ask him for directions, but, remember, my mouth was filling with blood, but I was sure, yes, I was sure he'd seen women in my condition & any moment now he'd recognize me. *You must be Puerto Rican,* he said & I wanted to cry ¡*Wepa, hermano, wepa! Ayudame, por favor. I knew it,* he said, *your hips & ass gave it away,* & he grabbed me & forced his mouth on mine.

He should've known & I didn't wish to save him, so I opened my mouth & he drowned.

In the Country Where
My Parents Met in a Taxicab

I was almost named after the woman
who put out a cigarette with her red high heel—
it's the carnival scene, John Travolta on his knees,
worshipping her black spandex pants and red-belted waist.
It was the first movie my mother watched in America.
She didn't speak English. I didn't

eat the beans from the school cafeteria.
They were never served with rice, just
a hotdog. But I learned
that an A in spelling equaled coupons
for free cheesy breadsticks at Domino's.
And I learned that hair
wasn't supposed to smell like fried pork chops
when the white kids formed a line
to whiff my braids.

When my cousin and I played American,
she'd grunt and move her tongue,
make weird sounds. I'd pretend
not to know English. Then we'd buy
too many things with Monopoly money,
stuff them into plastic bags.

When *Grease* came on TV,
my mother would hum the songs—
You're the one that I want, oo-oo-oo, honey . . .
My lips to the screen, I'd breathe
a name into the fog, the smoke
crushed under a foot.

The Association of Small Bombs
after Karan Mahajan

You destroy a city
   w/ what it provides.

Inject the city's veins w/ hives of buzzing
    drunks littered along the freeway's trash
     until they are heaps of rusted aluminum.
Until they are serrated
   teeth waving knives at shadows.

They sit on corners—
    imbalanced Buddhas w/ decks of cardboard tarot.
They are the prophets of losses,
    unfortunate tellers extolling the quiet
      neon hum of dying.

You blow up a city
   w/ what it provides.

Train clandestine meth heads
    to build rockets in Motel 6 bathrooms.
Those crystalized scientists,
    baptizers of bathtubs,
      astronauts of vapor,
    their minds drowned in oxidized drains.

We're all fragile shrapnel, ground then snorted,
    glass pipe bombs embedded in the city's lungs.
Every breath cuts deeper,
    as we wait to explode.

You defile a city
   w/ what it provides.

The gritos of tías singing groserías
           calling in the wild
                     before night fall.
Their ambient epithets
           whispering dog whistles
                     reminding us to heel;
the echoes of shouts like ghosts,
           trapped in homes
                     surrendered to asbestos.

Fill the city's mouth w/ dust.
Scrape the Westside's pipes for Leukemia,
           bottle the hard water laced in clouds,
                     chant for smog-heavy rain to choke
                     its corroded throat.

Let it die—gather its bones.

You rebuild a city
           b/c it provides:

pothole mausoleums w/ dead pigeons—
           we pluck feathers like guitar strings
                     & construct wings,
we patch fragmented cement w/ weeds
           until every sidewalk flowers to garden,
           until every avenue is an artwork—
                     lined w/asphalt tattoos,
                                dangerous as wound
           snakes selling venom by the vial,
we recycle our griefs—
           sew the tattered fabric
                     of family w/ spent needles.

Then a generation armored
           w/ hand-me-downs lift, w/ cuffed wrists
the harvest of concrete & helicopter lights.
           Feed the city the alley's happenings,
                     shape capes w/ plastic bags
                                to carry in the storm,
           soften its edges w/ broken-glass-dipped fists

in gravel-buried clouds of exhaled smoke,
   stoke the fire of sunset—

you burn a city
   that doesn't provide.

Music as Harlem

Inner city Blues on sale for white suburban youth.
Paul Moony said it best, "Everybody wanna be Black but nobody wanna be
 Black."
From backpack tribes on a quest to change demographics
to opulent pornographic violence and bulletproof vests.

What happens to a dream that's bought?
Is it refundable if it doesn't turn out to be what you thought?
Is it impeachable if hope was all you got for your vote?
Does it shine around the neck, demanding your oppressor's respect?
Does it hypnotize, spinning on tires, or pacify like welfare checks?
Does it take YOU out of poverty, only YOU, leaving poverty behind without
 YOU?

[Somewhere in Los Angeles]
This Poem Is Needed

She charges her ankle bracelet // From the kitchen chair
    & Sunflowers in the white wallpaper // Begin to wilt.

I wilt with them // Before my sister // & Her probation
    Officer [who comes over to the house unannounced]

Just as we're // Preparing dinner // & What're we supposed to
    Do now // Cook for him?! Invite him to eat with us??

•

I'm hacking the heads // From broccoli stems // & Pretending
    His body's spread across the cutting board // Ugh.

This officer keeps talking nonsense & nudging his eyes around
    The apartment // Looking for—drugs // Alcohol

Alchemy // My sister waits for him to leave & then begins to rant
    Ramble about // Her childhood // & How she used to be

Before house arrest // The confines of these plastered walls
    & Her monitored route to work // Where

Every corner has a cop // Coddling a liquor store // Protecting their
    Notion of *freedom* // My neighborhood eats fear.

•

Mothers are being // Handcuffed & harassed // Homes are being
    Crushed like cigarette butts // Everyone I know

Hates the racist police & wants a revolution // But we seldom
    Aim the gun // Have you heard // How the bullets sing

162   Their anthem // Throughout the body?? // It sounds like God
         Shutting the door—Bang // Bang.

                                        •

      When it's dinnertime in heaven // & your officer's knocking
         Ignore him sister— let the door bruise.

      Let the bears devour our enemies // We've no obligation
         To open ourselves // For those who do us harm.

Brothers Under the Skin
after Piri Thomas

I buried my brother alive
once, as a joke, with his head
burning and his tongue lissom.
North American now,
he had learned to land
a twang into any
syllable to its near
breaking. He mastered
even a Yankee English.
He had the last name,
the accent, the pass-
port, and the blue
contact lenses. I wondered
if he remembered,
he had our eyes first:
the color of syrup
sapped in the spring.
We used to sit at the mirror,
him braiding my hair
and calling us beautiful.

Mexican Heaven

all of the Mexicans sneak into heaven.
St. Peter has their names on the list,
but the Mexicans haven't trusted a list
since Ronald Reagan was president.

*

St. Peter is a Mexican named Pedro,
but he's not a saint. Pedro waits at the gate
with a shot of tequila to welcome
all the Mexicans to heaven,
but he gets drunk
& forgets about the list.
all the Mexicans walk into heaven,
even our no-good cousins who only
go to church for baptisms & funerals.

*

all the Mexican women refuse to cook or clean
or raise the kids or pay bills or make the bed or
drive your bum ass to work or do anything except
watch their novelas, so heaven is gross. the rats
are fat as roosters & the men die of starvation.

*

St. Peter lets Mexicans into heaven
but only to work in the kitchens.
A Mexican dishwasher polishes the crystal,
smells the meals, & hears the music.
they dream of another heaven,
one they might be allowed in
if only they work hard enough.

*

there are white people in heaven, too.
they build condos across the street
& ask the Mexicans to speak English.
i'm just kidding.
there are no white people in heaven.

*

tamales. tacos. tostadas. tortas.
pozole. sopes. huaraches. menudo.
horchata. jamaica. limonada. agua.

*

Jesus has a tattoo of La Virgen de Guadalupe
covering his back. turns out he's your cousin
Jesus from the block. turns out he gets reincarnated
every day & no one on Earth cares all that much.

*

it turns out god is one of those religious Mexicans
who doesn't drink or smoke weed, so all the Mexicans
in heaven party in the basement while god reads
the bible & thumbs a rosary. god threatens to kick
all the Mexicans out of heaven si no paran
con las pendejadas, so the Mexicans drink more
discreetly. they smoke outside where God won't
smell the weed. god pretends the Mexicans are reformed.
hallelujah. this cycle repeats once a month. amen.

Soy de la Luna / I Am from the Moon (Volveré a la Luna / I Will Return to the Moon)

for the two thousand three hundred immigrant children separated from their parents

I can count to two
thousand and three
hundred in two hundred and
thirty minutes.

Let me start with
mi'jo, mi'ja, mi vida, petunia.

My heart beats two thousand and four
hundred times in a half an hour.

Mi'jo, mi'ja,
mi vida, petunia.

I'll lose two thousand and three
hundred hairs in twenty-three days.

Mi'jo, mi'ja,
mi vida, petunia.

I'm trespassing once
I stop moving.

Mi'jo, mi'ja
mi vida, petunia.

The breath from my lungs is ninety
percent moon dust.
I can hardly breathe.

Mi'jo, mi'ja,
mi vida, petunia.

My heart broke the day my mother
told me I would
outlive her. I cried so hard
I couldn't breathe.

Mi'jo, mi'ja,
mi vida, petunia.

I dream of a bridge covered in lions'
heads, their tongues a full moon.

Mi'jo, mi'ja,
mi vida, petunia.

My blood has turned to wine.
I forget to breathe,
forget to look
for the moon.

Mi'jo, mi'ja,
mi vida, petunia.

The lilacs' bloom
doesn't last.
I see a girl turn into a fawn
the moon blocked by streetlights.
How awful to
hide those white
splotches, bits of
moon dust against
the grass too wet—wept with tears.

Mi'jo, mi'ja,
mi vida, petunia.

I carry the dark
of her eyes, the

168   recommended amount
of sodium is two
thousand and three
hundred milligrams
every day. Salt is
from the sea.
The sea's tide
is controlled by the
moon which says,
mi'jo, mi'ja,
mi vida, petunia.

The arctic tern
will bring back all two
thousand and three
hundred to the moon.
Each one flies that distance three
times during their life.
I trust them to carry
each mi'jo, mi'ja,
mi vida, and petunia home.

16

La Bandera

In Another Life

The war never happened but somehow you and I
    still exist. Like obsidian,
we know only the memory of lava
    and not the explosion that created

us. Forget the gunned-down church, the burning
    flesh, the cabbage soup.
There is no bus. There is no border. There is no blood.
    There are

only sweet-corn fields and mango skins. The turquoise
    house and clotheslines.
A heaping plate of pasteles and curtido waiting to be
    disappeared into our bellies.

In this life, our people are not things of silences
    but whole worlds bursting
into breath. Everywhere, there are children. Playing
    freely, clothed and clean.

Mozote does not mean massacre and flowers bloom
    in every place shoes are
left behind. My name still means truth, this time
    in a language my mouth recognizes,

in a language I know how to speak. My grandmother is
    still a storyteller although I am
not a poet. In this life, I do not have to be. This poem
    somehow still exists. It is told

in my mother's voice and she makes hurt dissolve
    like honey in hot water, manzanilla
warming the throat. You and I do not find each other
    on another continent, grasping

at each other's necks in search of home. We meet

in a mercado, my arms overflowing
with mamey and anonas, and together we wash them
	in riverwater. We watch sunset fall over

a land we call our own and do not fear its taking.
	I bite into the fruit, mouth sucking
seed from substance, pulling its veins from between my teeth.
	Our laughter echoes

from inside the cave, one we are free to step outside of.
	We do not have to hide here.
We do not have to hide anywhere.
	A torogoz flies past my face

and I do not fear its flapping.

La Tribu Sabe

Nigga, everything the Black girl does, is BLACK
She breathe BLACK
She talk BLACK
She dress BLACK

*Like the omen
this is for my homie
and you know me
for makin' niggas so sick*

Queen Bee, BLACK, no bleach
Queen Bey, BLACK, no blonde
Fox Boogie, BLACK, no brown

*I raised you
basically, made you*

Red lip on deck, by birthright
Red lip on dick, by choice
Shut up when it's Black-girl hour
When it's bruja-heavy
Santera.

*Dear, God. If you're here
God. Make the fire
disappear when they stare
God. Take away my fear / when they interfere, God.*

Black girls be:
Salt in open flesh wound
Flesh wound
Open
Sea of agony
Slayed for the gods
Oyá

*Do you fear God?
Cause I fear God*

Bendición, Black girl

> *Que Dios te Bendiga,*
> *Black girl*

As-salāmu 'alaykum, Black girl

> *Wa'alaykumu as-salam,*
> *Black girl*

Alhamdulillāh, black girl
Alhamdulillāh, Black girl
Alhamdulillāh, BLack girl
Alhamdulillāh, BLAck girl
Alhamdulillāh, BLACk girl
Alhamdulillāh, BLACK girl
Alhamdulillāh, BLACK Girl
Alhamdulillāh, BLACK GIrl
Alhamdulillāh, BLACK GIRl
Alhamdulillāh, BLACK GIRL

> *La tribu sabe*[*]

---

[*] "It's All About the Benjamins (Remix)"—Lyrics by Kimberly Denise Jones aka Lil' Kim; "Ain't No Nigga"—lyrics by Inga DeCarlo Fung Marchand aka Foxy Brown;" Girl on Fire (Inferno Version)"—lyrics by Onika Tanya Maraj aka Nicki Minaj.

Mexican Bingo

My family won't let me play unless I call the cards in Spanish: la botella, el apache, el cantarito. We cover our cards with beans we can barely see against our skin, plop down tough little hearts of dirt that might split in our hands. We become clichés. My cousin Ruby strolls through the house in a black tube top, asking if anyone wants a tattoo in Old English. An ashtray brims with Virginia Slims & Kools butts, & weed we can't fit in the joint. My tía asks me to order the inmate package for Daniel. *Use Golden State Care, Mija, I heard from Rachel that they were the best.* I order ten Top Ramens and a pair of Nike Cortez for my cousin who lives in a box at Wasco. I can't help but think he's built it himself. We say our own names for the people on the cards. La chalupa is the hoe in the boat; el negro is my cousin's Oaxacan boyfriend, Sleepy; el soldado is my brother in Iraq; el boracho is my Tío Gilbert splayed on the couch, el corazón is my sister, the only reason my father does not leave; and el diablo, my mother says—that's me. No matter how many chances I get to correct, no matter how much my Tía glares, I cannot call the cards by their rightful names if I don't have one. We are both the el apache and la dama, the lost and the found. I have twice inherited one language and lost my atlas to the fifth dimension of Chicanismo. The words we never asked for make us illegible. Nights like this, I drink to remember the friar forcing my *r*'s with curled leather, the quiet god making my *a*'s a little dirtier. I reclaim mutilation, roll it like a velvet red carpet to the dining table, play the appropriator, play the priest but not the pocha, not here, just the halves of myself I never wanted to be. I know I'll be ashamed of it tomorrow. That's why I'm praying with my hands in my coat. That's why I throw the beans away every time.

School of Fish with Angel, New Edens
after Ficre Ghebreyesus

for Paradise, which burned in 2018

flurry of fish
scales effervescent in their glitter fields
frantic in their pooling to color the sea
what messages do they write
in tail swishes
the acrobatics of dive and float
food in the water
who swims and who drowns
only the muck knows their names
though the fish have tasted
a new salt in the swollen sweat
migrants in the loose tumble of water

here there is fire
that scorches paradise
and i ponder an abandoned school bus
charred shell
the windows blown out
and frozen in molten rainbowed glass
how beauty marks itself from shadow
ash and ember wastelands

in water and fire
there are schools
that teach us
paradise is a dream
and still we reach toward it
watched by angels
who weep behind
their firebrand swords

Marigloria Palma,

trans. Carina del Valle Schorske

amigo, esto que duele

(un poematón)

Puerto Rico es una bala hinchada entre mi pecho.
Es algo que me duele, que me seca el retoño.
Por su culpa soy trescientas bombillas
de ilusión apagada...
Antes tenía una fronda de campos exaltados,
un lucero amarillo temblando en el copete.
Pero antes yo era la retórica ciega.
Yo era un balón de gas con sombrero adornado;
un papagayo esléndido.
Antes yo no tenía un línea en la frente
ni un grillo zumbador en el cerebro.
Era una niña diáfana, era una niña alegre.
Yo era una risa nómada a lomo de camello
y mi conciencia era harina sin cocer.
Repicaba tambores por los largos pasillos
de la idea transitada. Lo que decían, decía
y lo decía más alto.
Iba en la procesión del aplaudido
o disparaba el grito derramando la espuma que contagia.
A la zaga del féretro, si lloraban, lloraba.
Y adueñada del hoyo, comandando el vacío
con la esbelta sonrisa como trigo esparcido
de mi puñado de tierra
que estrellaba la fosa.
En mi vida flotante, en mi ayer,
yo era mosca de papel barnizado.
Cada idea con peluca doblegaba mi cresta,
horadando los tímpanos de mi alma de cebolla
                        ¿infatuada?
Yo era entonces trescientas bombillas encendidas,
cero dimensionado, escalera que trepa.
Amigo, eso era antes, ahora todo me duele.

Me duelen las costillas rojas del flamboyán,
las palmas desahuciados, el mar con su epilepsia
tan azul y tan mío...
Me asesora el ladrido de una nueva conciencia,
un Puerto Rico silba en mitad de mis bronquios,
una ponzoña vierte veneno en mi sonrisa
y es un tiro de estrellas mi emoción controlada.
La otra y yo nos rompimos al mirarnos de frente.
Hubo aullido en los trámites...
Puerto Rico es cabeza de alfiler jorobado;
estrellita que flota en la risa convulsa y vedeazul
del océano. Su minuscule cuerpo,
                        su humildísima estirpe
lacera los ijares de mi enternecimiento.
Es que lo estoy pariendo cada cuarto de hora.
Lloro mi llanto agrio, siento mi grito híbrido.
Yo lo quería gigante, piafador, desdoblado
y es minúsculo beso de geográfico inválido.
Yo podría decir:
la palabra que nutra la verdad de un poema
endurece su magia. Yo podría gritar:
vengan treinta madonas con el pecho espumoso
a lactarle la esencia a la isla en el mar.
No lo digo, no basta.

Yo prefiero decir:
oye, puertorriqueño: cría dientes voraces
en la masa encefálica; alimenta tu vida con papilla
de ideas; enarbola la fanática unción del yo quiero y
demando, la esclavitud del puedo, la devoción elemental
de debo, el impulse adiestrado del conozco...
Puerto Rico es enano y será siempre enano en el gran
universo. Rompe la cruz infame en donde crucificas
tu devocíon al agro. ¡Hazte duro! ¡Hazte martir!
                        ¡Muere tu dulce muerte!
¿Debo decir y yo esto...? ¿ Y qué tal si dijera...?
Hay que halarle el ombligo a Puerto Rico,
adensar su cumbrera, echar bosque de ideas sobre
el bosque de hojas, fabricar con el seso la extensión
que nos falta. Abundar con la magia del pequeño
                        cerebro

178   los muñones sin piernas, mar afuera, alto viento
hacia el fuego sin macula.
Prolonguemos su carne con relojes y nervios, con afán
de martillo, con amor de habitantes,
                    con afecto de vástagos.
¿Tú me oyes, amigo? ¿Tú sientes la potencia que mi
voz desparrama? Mete tu hombre y empuja mi dolor
                    hacía
el cielo. Nos crucifica el mar, puertorriqueños...
¡Seamos incandescentes, incendiemos el mar!

Friend, This Is What Hurts

(a mega poem)

Puerto Rico is a bullet lodged in my chest.
It's what hurts me, what sucks my spring dry.
Because of Puerto Rico I'm three hundred
lightbulbs of illusion gone dead.

Before, I had a green frond from exalted fields,
I had a bright yellow star that trembled on the hilltop.
But before, I was nothing but blind rhetoric.
I was a featherhead with a fancy hat, a splendid parrot.
Back before I had a single line on my forehead
or crickets crowding my brain, I was a diaphanous girl.
Happy. I was a nomadic laugh on the back of a camel,
and my conscience was dry flour. I went drumming
down the long corridors of well-worn theories.
What they said I said, and I said it louder.
I used to follow the procession of applause, spit
contagious slogans. In the line behind the coffin,
I wept if they wept. I was master of the grave,
commandeering the void with a svelte little smile,
and the dirt I threw in the ditch was a fistful of cake flour
that dusted the darkness with stars.

In my floating life, in my yesterday,
I was a fly on flypaper. Every idea
with a wig on it made me grovel,
tunneling through the eardrums of my onion soul.
Infatuated? I was three hundred lightbulbs burning,
a zero in every dimension, a staircase tripping over itself.

But friend, that was before. Now everything aches.
The red ribs of the flame tree bruise me,
the chronic palms, the sea with its epilepsy
so blue and so much mine. . .

A new conscience barks at my heels,
Puerto Rico whistles my windpipe in two,

a tonic drips poison into my smile, and my heart
is a bottled storm of shooting stars.

We shattered when we faced each other.
There was a howling in the paperwork.
Puerto Rico is a hunchback pinhead,
a little star floating on the blue-green
convulsions of the ocean's laughter.
Puerto Rico's tiny body; her lowly race
strips the flesh from my tenderness.
It's just that I'm in labor every fifteen minutes.
I cry my bitter cry. My hybrid scream.
I wanted it huge, hoofs pounding out of me.
But it's a miniscule kiss of invalid geography.

I could say:
the word that feeds a poem's truth
makes its magic last forever. I could call down
thirty virgins with foaming breasts to nurse
us on the essence of the island-in-the-stream.
But I won't say it. It's not enough.
I would rather say:
listen, Puerto Rican. Let your brain grow
rapacious teeth and feed your life on the pulp
of thought, fly the fanatical flag of *I want*
and *I demand,* the slavery of *I can*, the elemental
devotion of *I must*, the educated instinct of *I know.*
Puerto Rico is a runt and will always be a runt
in the universe. Break the infamous cross
where you suffer for your devotion to the old farmland.
Make yourself hard! Make yourself a martyr!
                Die your sweet death!
Should I say such a thing?
And what if I do?

Puerto Rico: the cord must be cut.
Cast a forest of ideas over this forest of leaves,
let our senses see what we can't reach.
Extend the legless amputees
with the magic of our little mind,
the surrounding sea, high winds

whipping up a pure flame.
Let's prolong our flesh with clocks and nerves,
with the hammer's keening, the love of native species,
the sympathy of shoots and stems and leaves.

Do you hear me, friend?
Do you feel the power my voice proliferates?
Shoulder my pain and push it skyward.
Puerto Ricans, the sea will crucify us.
Let's be incandescent. Let's set the sea on fire.

On Nationalism

1. An erasure   (from Woody Guthrie's *This Land Is Your Land*, original 1940
      lyrics included)

This land is   land,   is land is   land
                            the   Island,
the   Forest,   the   waters,

            America
                        made
                        that   highway
And saw   endless
                        gold.

            America
                        made   me
    roam   and ramble and follow   footsteps
To   her diamond

            America
                        made

a high wall there   to stop me
A sign   said: Private Property,
                        it didn't say

            for   me

                                    I was
                        dust
            chanting   the
G-d America
            made

One morning
                                    I
    stood hungry,   wondering if

2.
America was not founded by immigrants.
Immigrants found America
and dropped the name on it
like
a drone.

I do not tout the phrase *we are all immigrants!*
because everyone is not one, some
were born here
well before the nation
was a nation,
just earth
brown enough to call a home.

I don't mind immigration. Just do it the legal way!
—said the offspring of a colonist.

I am not American
because I am "proud."
I am American
despite bombing seven countries,
despite exploited labor,
despite Palestine,
El Salvador,
Guam.

I do not need to wave an empire's flag
to prove I am deserving of a life.
I do not need a status nor a paper
to tell me who is or is not worthy of survival.

I cannot pride the nation
nor the journey required to arrive.
I cannot pride the heat
nor the drownings,
nor the waves of our bombs
punching entire families to the shore.

What I pride
is the day a sail grew out
of our grandmothers' backs
and a compass
from our G-dchildren's throats.

I pride a people
and their people
and all the sand
from which we dare
to rise.

3.
Humans are not G-d-fearing creatures.
G-d is a human-fearing creature. G-d fears
humans who fear other humans, and in this
way, human and G-d cannot trust each other.

Humans fear humans with G-ds not their own.
G-ds not their own become *no G-ds*. Humans
of no G-ds become *not human*, and in this way,
human and human cannot trust each other.

Human forms nation to touch G-d, and nation
Michelangelos the moon. But nation does not rule under G-d.
Nation rules with the hand of G-d, or sought to become G-d,
and in this way, nation and G-d cannot trust each other.

But the nation so blessed G-d, G-d soon became the nation. G-d
drapes the nation's face in every classroom, demands a prayer with each
sunrise. G-d tells Abraham to sacrifice his only son in Vietnam, in Kuwait,
in Iraq, and in this way, the oil and G-d may trust each other.

For nation does not rule under G-d. G-d rules G-d.
Nation rules under interest group, under
corporate investment, under capitol, and capital, and
in this way, the nation and AIPAC* may trust each other.

---

* American Israel Public Affairs Committee

For what acts of nation are not acts of G-d? What is a drone strike but a
flash of lightning from the sky? What ships have not turned water
into blood? What draft has not claimed the firstborns of entire cities?
And in this way, Raytheon and G-d may trust each other.

G-d democratized the world in eight days and extorted it nine. G-d poofs
a wedding caravan forgotten and calls it collateral. G-d substitutes
collateral with a stack of cash—G-d strikes a funeral procession,
and Forgotten mourns Forgotten becoming Forgotten,

and Forgotten forms its own G-d, and in this way,
Forgotten and G-d cannot trust each other.

La Orquesta Misión

Vecindad de paredes que cantan
en colores de fuego y sol
brillando como las manos
que tocan el tambor.

La orquesta de la misión
buena bomba, sabroso son,
el ritmo de estas calles
nacido en el corazón.

The cymbals are black lids
closing on a crescendo of trash
detailing the week's chorus.

An audience member greets the morning
by syphoning a big bottle into a little
liquor-to-go plastic miniature
because the day is speeding ahead
and he needs fuel.

The composer nods at the man
wearing a rainbow-patterned propeller hat
who chalks a river of soft pastels
on the possibility of blank pavement.

The boy and I step over watery lines
pointing the way. Echoes of a conch shell
reassure we are going the right direction,
despite the constant stream of strangers.

La orquesta de la misión
sabrosa salsa, rica cumbia
canciones de la gente
lo que forma este lugar.

In the distance, the timpani keeps

time with the bulldozers
ripping up asphalt and recuerdo.

The man who sleeps through
intermission dreams about clean blades
on his grass pillow, the green
planting-currency filling his pockets.

Blinds raise and swaying curtains strum
the man awake in time to avoid
the percussion section courtesy of the garbage truck.

A resonating bass closes the arrangement,
the abandoned couch remaining.
Having found some cash in his sleep,
the man offers to buy the audience
member a drink, on him.

They compare notes about pretend money
with a good exchange rate
and empty bottles that overflow.

Caminando y recordando
comunidad sobreviviendo
Alfonso con poesía,
y Chata, la música.

La orquesta de la misión
sabrosa rumba, siempre samba
nuestro espíritu
lo que forma este lugar.

La orquesta de la misión
buena bomba, sabroso son
el ritmo de estas calles
el ritmo de estas calles
nacido en el corazón.

Home
After Safiya Sinclair's "Home"*

have I forgotten it—wild conch-shell dialect / cave of captive

consonants beneath my tongue / how our words bloom

from the same backbone / *respirar* and *espiral* / our breath

of cyclical measures—to breathe here is an arrow / exhales flat

like fog—I practice sighing in spirals / fear not breathing

up storms / for is that breathing at all / return is too jagged

a shard to walk on / my soles have pinkened

and grown cays / scarred in islands / I swallow sea glass

hope the waters will tumble / and roll me a

shore lined in baygrape and Indian-almond / lips plump

with guinep and guava—I've sucked / on their pulp

and patience / savored floating halos of seaweed

and sorrow / eaten fistfuls of sand and sung

the slow-borne sadness / of island and exile—

and here I stand / still / at the edge of this mouth

this piercing pant / of a country / in perpetual weep

and rage and plight / for what is betrayal if not happiness

in a place not home / forgive this grieving body

remind it of laughter / roaring / *libre* / like waves

sloshing lilt / of churned salt and seafoam / of the sea

that again and again / I pray / does not forget my name

---

* "have I forgotten it—wild conch-shell dialect" was borrowed from Safiya Sinclair's "Home," as was "of the sea that again and again I pray does not forget my name." The latter underwent slight modifications.

Patria*
Inspirado por el poema "Home" de Safiya Sinclair

la he olvidado?—dialecto de caracola desatado / cueva de consonantes

cautivas bajo mi lengua / como nuestras palabras retoñan

de la misma vértebra / respirar y espiral / espiraciones

de medidas cíclicas—respirar aquí es saeta / suspiros planos

como niebla—practico exhalar en espirales / temo no resoplar

tormentas / es eso tan siquiera respiro / el regreso es astilla

muy serrada para caminar / la suela de mis pies se tiñe rosada

y brota cayos / cicatriza / en islas / trago vidrio de mar

esperanzada / que las aguas me revuelquen y rueden a

una costa forrada de uva de playa y almendro / labios rebosantes

con quenepa y guayaba—he chupado su pulpa y paciencia /

saboreado halos flotantes de alga y duelo / devorado puñales de arena

y cantado / la morosa tristeza de isla y exilio—y aquí me encuentro

parada / quieta / al borde de esta boca / de este perforante

resollo de país / en llantos y rabia y contienda perpetua—

qué es la traición / sino la felicidad / en un lugar que no es la patria?

perdona a este cuerpo desolado / recuérdale la risa / rugiente / libre

como olas / salpicada cadencia / de sal y espuma batida / recuérdale

la mar / que vez tras vez / rezo / no olvide mi nombre

---

* Esta es una traducción al Español por Ana Portnoy Brimmer del poema "Home," igualmente por Ana Portnoy Brimmer. Este poema y su versión en Inglés fueron inspirados por el poema "Home," de Safiya Sinclair, y toman prestado los versos, "have I forgotten it—wild conch-shell dialect" / "la he olvidado?—dialecto de caracola desatado" y "of the sea that again and again I pray does not forget my name" / "recuérdale la mar que vez tras vez rezo no olvide mi nombre", del poema de Sinclair (el último de estos dos versos siendo modificado ligeramente).

Our Big Bang

An African Dominican American Lion enslaved to forever Dodge Impalas,
Patron Saint of the Corner, blocking the bodega entrance.

Lion is taught in overcrowded schools
street-smart autodidact in perpetual in-school suspension
from detention to probation never on time, always doing time.

Lion is rehabbed in overcrowded prisons
where deadbeats reunite with sons,
and stepsons long to murder stepfathers and sex grandmothers.

A Street Fighter villain—an endangered species—like some American bison
hunted whenever outside the redlining around the reservation.

This lion is herded by pigs protecting property,
and then scalped and branded *felon*.

Lion suppresses the roar in his lungs
with cough syrup and a high-fructose corn syrup diet.
His reality dissolves like sugar in boiling water,
like opium poppy on a burning spoon.
The tension in his chest crackles
like baking soda on a frying pan.

Lion is raised where aimless gunshots are more punctual than sunrise.
Lion confuses murder with a starting gun
and a late start with fate.

Lion is ashamed of his Timberlands, scuffed like his criminal history.
broke and broken, daydreaming on the next "come-up," and new Timbs.
Lion is made up of song samples and the boom-bap in a DJ's diaspora inner-
    city mix,
Afro Americanized Taíno hick, tempted to get a fix whenever he recalls it's all
    fixed
and that he won't get a piece until the day it all explodes to bits.

Until one day the Lion remembers the roots
under four hundred years of cement.
While pouring cognac over concrete
spirits splash and stain his Timberlands forever,
but this time it's different.

Lion harnesses the love inside to slaughter a pig with its own snout,
and when the blood hits the Timberlands
that will be our big bang.

First Mourning

They kill my people
Ransack their lives
Leave them disheveled
Blaspheme their lush countryside

They kill my people
Sully their warm wind
Tattoo their skin with blood

They kill my people
Steal their mountains and clear skies
Take my people
To lonely cities to die

The power of their sun but a disfigured memory now

Areyto for the Shipwrecked

Chorus: Lost Articles   *First Voice: DREAMcatcher*

                The   Illegal my eyes. Iris of unfertilized
                        aliens   plateaus.   Unforgiven
                                                    for surging into a dialect
the   with no global market value.
                the   Illegal my argot. I cannot
the   just wade out in neutral lakes. I
        the   the   cannot say.   Cannot evade
                                            the plexus that marks me
                                            contraband.   When I seed above
        the   ores you crave you illegal me, forge
                an   deeds, uproot me,   hire me
                                                    to manage the waste,
the   illegal my soles   when your
                                            arsons drag me to your doorstep.
the   Illegal my faith.
                                            Broadcast me an illegal substance.
            the   Refuse me lodging   if I refuse
                        a   to be free   labor.
            a   Allege me vermin,   toxin,
                                                    zombify all kin who return
                                                    enraged by your
                the   tombopolis. Illegal my relics, confiscate
                                                my liver.   Now
                                            even my scars must be registered.
                                              Illegal my pyres   enkindled
                                            by your   rote pandemics.
                                                    Illegal the bronze of my
                                            cutis. If I split walnuts
                                            with the neighbors
                                                    somehow it's lascivious.
                                            Illegal my parchments, my pons,
                                                my corybantic time signatures.
                                            Only my silence   is welcome.
                                            Only my silence   is suspect.

Second Voice: Sleep Dealer (dir. Alex Rivera)

Dry, this mesa. What is potable siphoned
by drone shepherds warding these hinterlands.
Their lenses sniff me, hyper-poaching
company waves. Delete my source code,
spurring migration via system integration.
My rural gone obsolete. Bail to become

dermal conduit. Repurposed by coyote tech. Ahora soy
prosthetic stoop labor. Discarnate appendages uprooting

cassava via live stream. The innovation
this demesne of capital gain has sought:
an interface that un-Browns the goods.
Each hour spent beta-hitched to network
of cyber-maquilas surges my amaurosis.
Neural bandwidth atrophies when chains

go asomatous. Mi memoria outsourced to depleted
sectors, embezzled and greased to snooze pilferers.

Node-hunted. Ramsacked. My narcoprocessors
watt-sapped, until Luz hemo-hacks
wetware syncretism. Until metacarpal
of drone-shepherds hits ctrl+alt+del.
Hops mode and margin. Excises
ill logic gate that robohews granjero

from extranjero. Inducing BitTorrent deluge of ancient
rain to el campo. The file-swarm englutting me shunted.*

---

* "Lost Articles: A Migration Story" is an erasure of Section 6 of the Jones Act, "SALE TO ALIENS (46 App. U.S.C. 865 [2002])."

A Sermon on the Subway
and I Remember My Island

tumbling through tunnels / lights flicker / fireflies / in the seething stitches of / this city has yet to fear glass / I've known shards / softer than the edge of / empty / bulbs hang hushed from half-houses / and crumbling ceilings / on my island / no one asks for light anymore/ we've learned to suck on and savor / the dim / brittle like sacramental / bread sifts / through our fingers biblical dust / only the waters rise / and grow warm / like fresh loaves—

people only turn to god / when things go wrong / call on him / in times of trouble / and only then they ask / where's the light? where's the bread? / but god is / always here / and when the earth starts shaking / there's not one soul / that's gonna be able to stand / not one—

we call on god / in our goodbyes   *adiós* / name our children after him *Jesús* / suspended from our necks / between our breasts / pendulums / of piety / we carry the weight of him *amén*—why does the earth tremble / beneath us / when every day / like sackfuls of sand we spill over / onto this earth / with his name / blighted bark / in our mouths?

The Only Mexican

The only Mexican that ever was Mexican fought in the revolution
and drank nightly, and, like all machos, crawled into work crudo,

letting his breath twirl, then clap and sing before sandpaper
juiced the metal. The only Mexican to never sit in a Catholic pew

was born on Halloween, and ate his lunch wrapped in foil against
the fence with the other Mexicans. They fixed old Fords where my

grandfather worked for years, him and the welder, Juan, wagered
each year on who would return first to the Yucatan. Neither did.

When my aunts leave, my dad paces the living room and then rests,
like a jaguar who once drank rain off the leaves of Cecropia trees,

but now caged, bends his paw on a speaker to watch crowds pass.
He asks me to watch grandpa, which means: for the day; in town

for two weeks, I have tried my best to avoid this. Many times he will swear,
and many times grandpa will ask to get in and out of bed, want a sweater;

he will ask the time; he will use the toilet, frequently ask for beer,
about dinner, when the Padres play, por que no novelas, about bed.

He will ask about his house, grandma, to sit outside; he will question
while answering; he will smirk; he will invent languages while tucked in bed.

He will bump the table, tap the couch; he will lose his slipper, wedging it in
the wheel of his chair; like a small child trapped in a well, everyone will care.

He will cry without tears—a broken carburetor of sobs. When I speak
Spanish, he shakes his head; and reminds me; he is the only Mexican.

My Spanglish

The questionnaire asked me to indicate my primary language
I checked-off "other," and in big, bold, blue bubble letters wrote in
SPANGLISH!
My Spanglish carries a Gillette under her tongue,
ready to cut you if you say she is the sister of ghetto Spanish
My Spanglish drops the "s" and makes it "ma' o meno,'"
switches the "r" with "l" pa no "botal la suelte,"
trills her rrrrrrrs cuando tiene un pique rastrerrrrrro,
and if you question the placement of her accent marks
she will replace them with side-eye

My Spanglish gets in trouble for falling asleep in church
and winking at altar boys, climbs the fence at Highbridge
pool to swim after hours
My Spanglish burns her eyeliner with a lighter before applying it
My Spanglish can't stop sucking her teeth
My Spanglish knows the difference between
coquito and limber, pastelitos and empanadas, frío frío and piragua
Knows how to carry the weight on her thighs, not her shoulders
My Spanglish cooks farina, tembleque, habichuela con dulce, arroz con leche,
calls it comfort food

My Spanglish knows lemonade-tamarindo was a popular drink and it still is
Knows every Prince, Hector Lavoe, and Fernandito Villalona song by heart
My Spanglish wants to be called sexy, not cute
My Spanglish wants to be called smart before sexy,
wants to be called beautiful like the blanquitas her ex parades
around the hood to show how he has moved up and on

My Spanglish mends her broken heart with bachata corta vena de Frank Reyes
se emborracha con boleros del Buki
My Spanglish always claps when the plane lands safely
My Spanglish thinks freca, presentá, y malcriá are all compliments,
married her cousin to help him get his green card,
doesn't let her kids sleep over anyone's house
My Spanglish has crooks and cops sitting at the same table

at her daughter's quinceañera
My Spanglish has a college degree and earned summa cum laude
in resting bitch face while riding the 2 train

My Spanglish is Washington Heights before the gourmet
fruit markets replaced C-town,
before tomándose una fría in front of el building playing
dominó con los panas was loitering,
before the *New York Times* and transplants from Minnesota
discovered pegaó on BuzzFeed and renamed it "stuck pot rice"

My Spanglish is Inwood before it became more affordable than
Williamsburg and was renamed Northern Manhattan
My Spanglish spray-painted over billboards trying to rename
el condado de la salsa "the piano district"
wonders if it would have made more sense to name us
"the bomba y plena district," "the home-of-hip-hop district"
or "the boogie-down district" but my Spanglish is certain
The Bronx has always been and will forever be ART!

My Spanglish knows a fire escape is also a terrace
My Spanglish knows there is no way to heal without
sana que sana culito de rana,
can't tell stories about el campo in translation,
can't flirt using proper grammar
My Spanglish knows there is no other way to say
Cónchole papi, you look good!

My Spanglish has a tía sin papeles
My Spanglish has a tía that works in a factoría
My Spanglish has a tía that takes care of neighborhood carajitos
My Spanglish will never call herself broken

My Spanglish is an unwanted child who insisted on being born
She is huérfana crying an unpaid debt of commonwealth
to mainland lost in a promesa
Leche cortá of impoverished madre patria and starved island retreat
She is the unruly second-generation daughter of
un-American and un-standardized
She is the endangered tongue of a sanctioned homeland and un barrio cabrón
My Spanglish is always trying to create a bridge connecting

My Spanglish is a scared seven-year-old in an English-only class where
Ms. Marcy tells me to sit in a corner every time my tongue
resists pressing *ju* into you and *jes* into yes,
insisting Mami's homemade lonches are better than cafeteria food,
certain that standing on el rufo is the only place I have ever seen stars

My Spanglish has an abuelito whose primary language is storytelling
but she doesn't have the time to sit and listen
My Spanglish can't understand all his consejos
but feels exactly what he means
when he says, *Te amo, te amo all the way*

Black on Both Sides

child of	rice and peas and
god	a bird sealed in oil
mother dressed	brown skin
for praise dance	platanos cooked
like	sweet
sunday's best	a cabinet full of
big hats	condensed
in every color	sugar
we listened to	grandma's patties
gospel on the sabbath	fingertips pinched
in prayer what held	the dough shut
us around the table	like a wound
was it faith or	learning to heal
an older dread	between our hands
grandma's skin	thighs breasts wings
so pale	white meat
at her funeral we knew	the table full when
she wasn't there but	the aroma called us
home	to eat
amongst the angels	before our eyes

Roatán

Seaside houses sitting on stilts and the kerosene lamps at night carried by my
grandfather.

The feral roosters gathered to sing in the sun sometimes.

(In the same yard: the cats stalk the chickens.)

At night, once, my father took me to see his old ship.

(Who said the ocean sounds like the clang of a bell?)

How did the seafloor not rise up?

(Have I not mentioned my grandmother?)

In the morning, the tilting schools of fishes, the rococo coral, and the sea salt,
sea salt colored everything.

(Pitch black when you open your eyes, so you think you are still sleeping.)

Sea turtles in confinement that were bound for soup.

Coconut bread, buttery fish sauce, and crab meat slipping out of cracked legs.

Our bodies should burst into rain.

The sky today is a kingdom of cumulus clouds.

(What are the places we go to when we think of the end?)

"Ponele Queso Bicho"
Means "Put Cheese on It, Kid"

for Miguel Alcántara, aka La Belleza

¿Why you post on my fence and wait for water, Belleza?

> ¿You don't know? I'm Rambo.
> Look at these muscles, they shine like desks.
> Va. Call me Sevestre Escalon.

It's pronounced Sil-vés-tre, Belleza. Sil-vés-tre Es-ta-lón.

> Comé mierda bicho. I made the best desks.
> I had a shop. Ponele queso,
> every night I cut where branch meets trunk.

¿When you gon make me a desk then?

> I made desks. Ponele queso.
> ¿You know what that means?
> When I die my phrase is gon be on TV,
> it'll be like Sevestre in that movie *Cobra*.
> He'll try to figure what that shit means.
> Puta bicho, I'll be famous.

It's Sil-vés-tre, Belleza. And yes, I know what it means.

> ¿What it mean then?

Sounds like those mazes with the cheese in the middle and a rat outside.

> Va. Va. Va. You do use that coconut.
> I knew you were your father.

¿You knew my father?

> Don't touch the tiger's balls.

I made the smoothest desks. Ponele queso.
It's all in the smell bicho.

¿Did my father say that?

You're touching the balls. You're touching the balls.
But look, it's something like when you go to the store
and vodka is two colones ¿right?

Right.

The label says 80 proof. But rubbing alcohol is one colón,
200 proof. So I wait for you to bring water.

¿What does that mean?

Look, I was passed out when he got in that van.
He had a backpack. You were asleep. He didn't want to go.
But the dólares and war bicho. Ponele queso.
Ponele queso and the rat won't leave.

Hacha Bop

> *Fuerte, fuerte,*
> *Hacha y machete*
> —Héctor Lavoe

In the time of cutbacks and of kickbacks,
of congressmen waiting for their callbacks,
lobbyists cooing from their hatchbacks,
fronting the protectorate of greenbacks,
they tweet and blog to falsify the playback:
One nation strong? You're wrong. You want my feedback?

Fuerte, fuerte,
Hacha y machete

That's right, the Caribs knew the way to payback:
off with their skins, ask questions later. You just kick back
and tell stories of invaders who never made it back
to Europe. Go hatchet job somebody else, your market logic blown back
across choppy seas now blood-red. You've got it ass back-
wards if you think revenue-sharing works. Back
up. Look out. There are sharks in the back-
water. All banks are blood banks. Goldman Sucks. No thanks. You take it back.

Fuerte, fuerte,
Hacha y machete

Albizu knew machetes, Clemente with a k leading us back
to powder kegs in canefields like Césaire's. Islands brought back
into focus in the truth of Brown bodies in class scarfare. Bach
don't play here. Lavoe will holla back
from the jíbaro fields: blues, sones, prison toasts. No back-
track. Slave-ship spillover. The struggle makes us whole. No turning back.

Fuerte, fuerte,
Hacha y machete

Pantoum for Puerto Rico
after Hurricane Maria

Should my beaches ever
be stained with blood,
I could say the world
saw it coming all along.

If home is not bloodstained teeth
and a taste for vengeance,
it is seeing what has been coming all along
and having the arms open to hold it.

If home is not vengeance
against those who will not house us,
it is having the arms to hold all who are open season,
a red dot resting on a feast.

If home is not a house,
it is the vanished roof.
It is a dinner plate resting under a red dot.
It is the hunt that comes with the blood.

If home is not a roof,
it is the power outage.
It is the blood that cannot be hunted.
It is the lost cousin that was always lost.

If home is not power,
it is the storm.
It is the hurricane wall stealing your cousin's walls.
It is the nurtured natural disaster.

It is the storm.
Should my beaches ever be stained with blood,
it is the nurtured natural disaster
we saw coming all along.

Fiesta de los Palos

Palo music surges from the black-hole
       mouth of a mountain summoning spirits
from "el mas allá," and it resurrects the negra in me.
I ring-around-white-rose-petals that shake the center
   of my beating feet. Saints swirl in the spaces between
our palms. A maraca blows out the light of a candle.
The ay, ay, ay of a yellow-eyed woman wraps me
   in amaryllis and sage smoke. The inside of a Catholic
church never felt this holy. Knees and shoulders tug
and bounce to the rhythm of a drum—unsure of where
   I'm going but it must be somewhere my blood has been.

I cannot stop this shaking.

Bristles of history billow beneath my skin. La güira shakes
   and scrapes the hands of an ebony man who could be
my abuelo. My sweat becomes agua bendita.
My curls a double-swing machete blessing this palo fiesta
   with frankincense and myrrh. I bow my head
and arch my back—my body an altar for phantom
   memories that itch beneath the skin.

Notes on Pasteles

Tetris blocks of gold hide in the corners of December
each piece a tribute to my late wela

Rubber bands squeeze the pasteles
into stacks of money the whole block tryna stain

but a safe like this only opens with Bendiciónes
oozing from the mouths of those who have kissed every ancestor goodbye

When Jenny's bank account froze before Christmas
Mom folded masa until her hands dried in prayer

the dirt-brown mush seeped through the aluminum foil
and signed its name across the walls of the freezer in sacrifice

& what do you know about gold that runs and boils by the river
leaving nothing but a smell to trace our way back home?

Confessions on Gratitude

My father tells me of Chihuahua, his birthplace, of women selling roses on
street corners to remain alive, of children washing cars or selling mangoes with
no shoes. He tells me how he came to the US when he was ten, of how lucky he
was to obtain a green card from his father's new wife, how his father obtained
one from his boss. He tells me of the rotting car he drove from Arizona to
Boston, how lucky he was for it to not break down, how it was here where
he would meet my mother, find a job, have children, how everything I am, I
am because of good luck. And I am to be grateful for my existence, sure, but
sometimes, I wonder if Chihuahua is the greatest exporter of good luck. Bad
luck never gets anywhere. Bad Luck always drowns in the Rio Grande or is shot
halfway up the fence by an immigration officer, but good luck—Good Luck
gets the affirmative action scholarship. Good Luck applied for citizenship at the
right time.

I do not believe anyone died because they were not strong. I believe I survived
because I was lucky. I am lucky because the indigenous woman forced to bear
me staring down the eye of a Spaniard's gun did not end herself before starting
me. I am lucky because my Jewish family fled Russia before the raids began,
>   because my Jewish family fled Poland before the raids began,
>   because my Jewish family fled Spain before the raids began,
>   because my Mexican family's green cards arrived
>   *after* the raids began,
>   and I do not get to disassociate myself
>   from those who are undocumented
>   just because I have the fortune of being documented.

I am not joyful for Good Luck. Good Luck implies the death of everyone
who does not have it. I cannot celebrate Good Luck in a graveyard. I blow
out the birthday candles, and each year I survive is a year someone did not. I
walk to school *un*-bombed. I go to bed *un*-deported. I hit the bar *un*-droned.
I am everything the ground / did not bury. I want a victory out of this, but I
don't know what candles to offer the ghosts beside me. I want a cake, a party,
balloons, a gift basket. I want it all / entering the earth / when they did. I am to
be grateful for my existence, sure, but gratitude is a Cold War's reparation away
from justice. Gratitude does not lift up the dead, does not spill the life back into

a mother. I want to be alive and well and joyous, but if I knew the world like a cousin, I'd know death like a twin.

There is a boy / somewhere / with my name /
and he does not get to write this poem. /

I write this poem / because I am not him, /
but here, / alive, / so lucky.

Praise Dance at Utuado

i was last found
joy-tumbling in a ring of stones
to three trombones
harmony

of stabs
i am pierced   sheet music
under vanishing amber
leering upward

pleading a fall
to pour out
tributary of picked scabs
procession of lumbering clouds

border the altar   my bones in rare formation
I remember stumbling
through these steps before   cool-breeze naked
early wind   winged

callusing
coiling toes   bone now
worn and barrel
rolling   under an aguacero

downpour   soil over-
flowing from my toenails
river sloshing
in prayer   pruning

summoned storm
I have wept to life   once
I wore ruby feathers and
preferred the sky   now   I am

bended knees   blink flood
I see beyond this place   where clouds
gather   bend me a rain
and maybe   I'll go away

If I Ever Taste My Native Air

If I ever taste my native air,
I promise I will ignore the splinters
stuck between the saltwater particles,
and whatever grains of sand might be left
in the wake of Maria and her lungs,
full of Boricua breath and leveled towns
and her eye, blessed in the sight of elsewhere.
A body full of bodies begs of home.

Maybe we all look for some ground to touch
and say, "this is mine, and I am hers."
Is an embrace not a storm of wanting,
or but a way of circling back?
If el campo should ever come to me,
I promise I would be a storm at home.

This Being the Last Tree

for Peter Dolores Ayala Sepúlveda

A Boricua is born from the roots up
to study the light of the universe,
the Earth's drum, imbuing feet
with rhythms only the wind can carry,
only another Boricua knows.
He is given the cycles
of the land he broke with
for a different kind of freedom.
They are heavy soursop, bombing
the rubble with milky sweetness
to spite the windowpanes of the city,
this sky that can take us.
They joint his mind against the urban wind
like the nodes of sugarcane.
This being the last tree, his laughter
bounding from the last
airport of his imagination—
another Boricua is born of it
from the roots up.

Shithole Song #1106

we sing it in the blood flowers and we sing it while they bury our sisters

we sing it to the hungry rodents they cage us with

we sing and we sing and there are cannibalized families in the shithole

and the authoritative bodies dig and they say thank the lord we do not live in this
shithole where the babies cry for their cages   where the mothers have numerical
codes stitched into their skin   where the hole is overwhelmed by the shit
and the shit is overwhelmed by the hole   where the hired help helps the hiring
hands to rehumanize the exiled bodies whom they shovel into the shittiest shit
of the shithole

we are the moses and the aaron of the shithole and we sing this song of hope

we are the mannequins and the glass dolls of the shithole and we sing this song of
hope

we are diseased bits of shithole earth on lizard corpses and when our children
cry they tell us dig that shithole deeper

they say sing this song of hope and dig that shithole deeper

we sing it to the dead who drink our dirty shithole water

we sing it to the dead who sleep with the ghosts

in our hepatitis hole

in our meningitis hole

in the hole where they hide us like a debt that will never be paid

in the hole where they draw an intractable border through our broken
shithole bodies

the early americans tape up our eyes because God tells them to tape up eyes

they chain up our legs because God tells them to chain up legs

they gag our mouths because God tells them to gag our rotten shithole mouths

they put our children in cages because God tells them to put children in cages

they dig the shithole deeper because God tells them to dig the shithole deeper

they slaughter a few grandmothers because God tells them to slaughter a few
grandmothers

heaven is warm bread on every table

heaven is slow breath natural light warm bread on every table

in the shithole we have no bread and we have no table

we are the conquest of the shithole

and the reconquest of the shithole

and the counterconquest of the shithole

and our bodies possess collective resonance because we know that the global
economy cannot function without the shit and the hole of the shithole

we know the global economy cannot function without the song of hope
we sing to the shithole

we sing into the devices they hook to our bodies

we sing and we sing and sometimes they throw crumbs for us to fight over

rain falls into the shithole and they tell us we don't get wet

we are soaking wet but we are not wet because they say we are not wet

we are not wet because God says we are not wet and there are more
shitholes hiding in this shithole

they hide our passports in the shithole beyond our shithole

they organize our hunger into units of betrayal in the shithole

soon our shithole will be exported into a less shitty shithole in the prettiest
shithole of all the shitholes in texas georgia florida nebraska illinois
and new york shithole

we are the prettiest shit in the shithole

we are a people of hope and we sing and sing

we sing as they shit into our shithole

we sing as they shock us in the shithole

we sing at night as they lend us money to rent back our bodies in the shithole

we are proud to be a people of hope because they tell us we should be proud to be a
people of hope

and we sing the song of shithole hope as the souls of our slaughtered classmates fly
above our heads

we sing the song of shithole hope as the souls of our slaughtered nurses fly above
our heads

we sing the song of shithole hope as the souls of our slaughtered neighbors fly
above our heads

we sing the song of shithole hope when they shit into the shit of our shithole

we sing the song of shithole hope when they shove poison stones into our wound-
mouths

we are the slaughterers' nostalgia in the shithole

we are the murmuring wound-mouths of the rotten bodies that have been blown
apart in the shithole

we are the obliterating blankness of the shithole

we sing our song of hope to the massacring minds of the obliterating blankness
of the shithole

you are responsible for your wounds   says the authoritative body to the murmuring
wound-mouth in the shithole

and you are responsible for your children's wounds

and this is so because I say it is so

and I say it is so because God tells me it is so

and God tells me it is so because I am on the outside of the shithole and you are
on the inside

and on the inside of the shithole you are responsible for your wounds and for the
wounds of all your shithole family

you will be billed for your wounds when the entrepreneurial slaughterers of
the morning locate the polytheistic profit in the spiritual marketplace of your
ugly shithole mouth

because in the shithole   the death of the dead does not die

because in the shithole   the wound-mouth is stuffed with celebration cheese and
celebration wine

the wound-mouth is stuffed with the impossibility of feeling the feelings one feels
when one cannot contain their shithole feelings

here cometh the form of the shithole

and we sing

protect the concrete from the feet that walk it.   cover the concrete with pictures
of the bodies blown apart by the morning.   convince the bodies in the shithole
that the slaughterer is not a person

convince the bodies in the shithole that those they slaughtered are martyrs
sacrificed in the communal fight for eternal shithole justice

the river is dying   says the authoritative body to the shittiest shits in the shithole

the immigrants are flying   says the authoritative body to the shittiest shits in the shithole

the death of the dead does not die

Gangsta Bitch
for Cardi B

Bitccccccccchhhhh
            May I call you bitch?

We, daughters of asphalt,
flinching credit scores,
quivering language, became
big-bodied baby girls. Pigtails
on cubic zirconia skull chain
slung across broad chest,
can't hug pillar of man through glass.
We know betrayal sounds like
snitch of a metal detector,

            if a bitch beef
with me we gon beef forever

& if you love him you gon love him
foreva.
Regularshmegulardegular girl,
extraordinary heavy-handed love,
big soft heart & knuckle teeth,
chest cracked open,
left you bleeding in the middle,
leaking through the streets,
whispering your name through
sewer, concrete; you part your lips to say

            "dick sucking
        contest I'm winning."

Like only a gangsta bitch could.
Ready to rumble for your love,
hand-to-hand combat
to keep away bops and these curses
know you pray like you rap

all chest and pain.
You married his ass
for his dick & god.
Stripper turnt rapper
turnt over ass-up face-
down the years your girls
became bobblehead eye rolls.
Snakeskin stretching across their toes,
you know slithering looks like
Bitches hip-rolling next to you in the club.
Got you scared to trust anyone
But Hennessy.

God chose me and you. They   should figure it out.

But I been meaning to ask: you ever get
tired of anointing? You ever wish you
wasn't so holy, so sacred, so the apple of
God's eye that everyone waits for you
to go rotten?
When you felt the spirit jump out yo' body
and through yo' chancla, jimmy choo,
I wonder if you regretted dreaming this big.
Crazy how we
love the hood 'til the hood show up.
You all neck-roll
smacked lips, slick ponytail
scissor, eye-roll spotlight,
brown eyes—

bitttttttchhhh, I see you.

Mutt Life

who knows who she is I
keep the bitch on a leash
when we walk all night
I dream I have a spare
self to cage and bone
my bitch I do with her
whatever I won't

Otherness
(or, To the Side-Chicks of the World)

(This is not a poem about the Other,
entrenched in its flamboyant discourse.
No.
This is a poem about fucking.)

I am but the shadow of what you wanted it to be.
The sounds that echoed in that room
—long ago
—a year—
it diluted,
came apart, the seams burst open
—or wore off
—or soaked and festered, too
much flesh to put in a single room, honey i—
among the streets, down they ran,
    the steps
        we took in the
Santa Lucía.

Este no es un poema del Otro,
ese de los libros,
el de Said y Bhabha y Spivak,
ese que toma forma de sus bocas
y se traspasa hilando las páginas.

No. Este no es ese Otro.
I am not that Other.

Yo soy la *Otra*, y punto.
La que te tiraste en moteles,
con la que te cagaste de la risa,
a la que le refutaste todo,
la que era *good with words*,
las mismas que *chamuscaste* entre tu lengua y su piel
y devolviste luego arcanas y extranjeras y llenas de culpa y sexo y

La que te rompió *en teoría* el corazón.

Yo soy la vampira, la otra,
en toda su perra gloria,
el súcubo eterno de la noche.
El fruto que perdió el gusto
una vez probado
—te das
cuenta? La ficción
siempre
es mejor.

Y si soy ese Otro—hoy, lejos con la piel en contraste
las estaciones que nos separan—
me hizo así tu mirada
tu sudor tu calentura el cemento del Gran Santiago
el centro el café las piernas
tus ojos secos y nuestras cicatrices.

Y ella?
La otra, la con minúscula.
La real.
Ella, en su blanca ignominia,
inadvertida,
planea, teje, deshace la mortaja.

The Red Dress

What is it about a red dress,
that snaps a head back like an overstretched rubber band?

I only put on my red dress,
when I want to be the bloodshot pool in the center of your iris.

When I know there is nothing to lose,
 only eyes to steal,
  hours of time to put back into my dripping hourglass.

Slip the red dress on,
and the night's heartbeat throbs at the nexus of my index finger.
 Yeah in the red dress every move I make is photographed,
  each picture framed onto the fireplace of my exes.

  A rate of five hundred dollars is charged for each shot
  & deposited directly into my bank account-

      with the money, I buy
      ten more red dresses
      & live 200 more years.

In the red dress   me mando yo.

In the red dress every man that ever left me waiting   asks me to
 dance.

226   In the red dress   my mouth drops the word "no"

like a glass of wine   on your favorite   blouse.

In the red dress tears are a lake mirage to my pupils,

        I only laugh to show the size of my teeth.

                        In the red dress I hunger for oxygen like flame,
                                engulf every centimeter I find.

Hell's honorable showpieceyou can call me   here to bite back the night

here to claim everything stolen

mine.

Coming for the Throne:
Ursula's Love Story

When two women make love,
tridents lose their teeth,
dissolve into the foam of their lovemaking.

We are raised to love that which we are not,
to take a knife to our fins and sculpt feet,
to walk on blades, shave our scales
and pretend we are not dying of thirst.

When women choose the water
they choose their own reflections,
and nothing is more powerful
than two women in love.

There are no fairy tales written for us,
no love songs except the ones we sing of ourselves,
no story told a hundred times to lead the way,
or wreaths of seaweed at our wake.

Instead, we are called witch,
our abundance grotesque,
something to be controlled, destroyed
all because we do not need you.

Perhaps we are feared so much because
if there were too many of us
the oceans might grow too plenty,
and so much of this place is already water.

Self-Portrait as My Ancestry, La Malinche

The taco stand that used to be a Checkers
used to be a fruit stand, which used to be just
the land.

In every version I find something
worth consuming.

Doña Marina sold out her country
to Cortes, or Malintzin's own country
sold her—

Either way, La Malinche gave birth
to something new.

My father says his sister disappeared
with some boy. His mother says the man
disappeared with her.

Either way, she was never seen again
by anyone who knows me.

My mom says it's all the same story
told be different people. I say my parents
named me Malinchista—

So, I don't know what I own. I know that
I am loyal to whatever I can say is mine.

Dios te salve, Maria

la virgen de guadalupe loves me,
even though i'm queer. actually
la virgen saw a golden prayer of herself shimmer
around my neck when i was three months old and
made me gay.
she supported all my crushes,
even if she doesn't remember all of them.
some too straight, some too american to pronounce.
but la virgen loved all my daydreams about girls,
would never let me trip chasing them, or
made sure i had enough dollars in my pocket
to buy them a paleta. if she approved of the girl,
maybe two paletas, *para no chinges*.
i always kept la virgen on my neck,
a shrine to my day one.
la virgen gave me enough data
to download the app "her" and
the courage to tell my best friend
i was in love with her. in fact,
la virgen got tired of all my love letters stuck
in the back of my throat and whispered
in my best friend's ear, *ay,*
ella está enamorada de ti.
ask her, dame una risa and boom,
i had a girlfriend. that night i prayed to her,
"dios te salve, maria, la virgen, no you didn't, i mean,
mi reina, gracias" and she said,
no problem, pendeja.

The Future Is Lodged
Inside of the Female

passive tense because who did the lodging
or was it self-inflicted lodging? victim
is suffering. victim pronounced dead on arrival.
lodge big. lodge for the forgotten ones. lodge like it's 1995.

would be nice to advance & update but i'm just not feeling it today!
also then i can't claim to be marginalized so uh whatever.

in the future, i am not Spanish or Latina or Latinx instead i am:

H I S (P A N I C) <u>E D</u>

-ED because past tense because colonialism. as in, my identity is something that
    happened to me.
-PANIC to acknowledge crippling anxiety lol

here is a haiku:

somewhere in the world
there is a cishet white man
apologizing

that *is* a haiku & i *will* get the attention I deserve.

i want to turn the meat sack i live in into something more efficient
something that pops up toasted bread & tells you what's trending today

how many ways can i pull off my brand?
i have tweezers, sharp keys, an x-acto knife.
i'm okay with living
with the gaping wound & then the scar tissue & the story to have prepared
when people point & say
what happened there?

my work is all puns stapled together into the shape of a woman
who is really listening to you & laughing at all the right times.

i'm sorry this isn't about my mom's accent enough
or the way my father dilutes it.
i'm sorry this isn't about the ten occurrences of microaggressions i can think of
    off the top of my
head,

(are you with him or the cleaning service?)
(i'm just as dark as you in the summertime.)
(you're smarter than the other Latinos in this class.)

okay so maybe, like, three?

another haiku:

somewhere in the world
Lena Dunham is naked
apologizing.

my bad, you asked me to make this more *political* & *aggressive*
so i'm turning the phrase "it's up to you. i'm down for whatever" into a machete
& hacking at an ATM until i can pay the train fare it took me to get here.
    thanks!

realizing that all my life i've been trying to look like Selena? is Selena the hole
    that's been
carved out for me? i can jam my body through it but i'll probably fall to the
    other side. is my
body Selena-adjacent?

the female is twenty-three, hispanic(ed), with a bullet wound to the back.
the female is forty-five, hispanic(ed), crying in her car with a gun.
the female killed her best friend, because only one woman can exist at a time,
    whoops!

honestly so sad that she's dead but like, what if she lived long enough to like a
    tweet from a pro-
life organization.

232   i am deep inside now, with my fists, no gloves on!
      i am doing everybody a favor!
      the future is right past my reach & the size of a walnut!
      the future is an illusion & we are
      stuck picking our fingernails in the present. the future snores in my neck &
         loves me back!
      no, that is too much to ask of the future!
      yes, the future thinks about other people! you can't stop that!
      the future is in my hands now & won't stop making noise!
      can someone help me turn it off? please.

      my last haiku, i promise:

      somewhere in a room
      i'm saying *sorry, so sorry.*
      for no good reason.

Born Year of the Uma

Scuffing our sneakers on crumbled
blacktop, basketball courts dog-calling
Hialeah-hollering I say *Is there anything
more*
than Corey being born
in the year of the faggy Horse? Bitchass.
We cackle loud enough to light crows off
telephone poles & of course it's really me
who's ashamed of being horse-born year
after upended year still star sign of the
discolored stallion, me who is faggy, my
bitchass

clings saddle-tight & nightly dream
to my mare She is brown my
mare so brown as turned earth my nude
body blending perfectly paint-wet
across her bumpy spine ropes of her
dark mane malting against my small
chest I lay awake most nights
her dreaming like me to
crossover the shoals of some fairy-tale
body of river racing muddy through
field of green after
green

But I grow hand over hand sixteen hands
longer than the muscled trunk of her & in the
illness of my youth fading I beg to be reborn
year of the Ox

huffing gold clouds misted in tall grass with
horns long enough to hang the worries of my
small worlds or begat by Tiger years of
cleaning manblood from my claws snagged
dewy through green stalks reaching long as

234   earth's static hair for the underbelly remake me
in the image of the great red god of a dragon
the years I prayed to spit fire to sling fangs to
fly far from the black hearth of yet another
abusive boy's home

When finally I dream again of her my
mare she is dead. There is nothing but
a paling body a corpse spilled oilslick
in the dirt So I skin her I quarter her I
pack her tough meat to sell on street
corners Because O I have grown for
so long long look at me & my claws
of the Tiger how I flayed her long like
the horns of the Ox how I speared her
long like the fangs of the red god how
I devoured her Finally ruthless I am

with the
heart
of a
Dragon

to be
unmade
not long
for

Reasons Men Build Walls

My lover fears me.

There is too much cumbia,
    too much Selena in my walk.

    Too much Frank Ocean in my lovin',
        too much storm in our summer kiss.

I am too-much-sugar-pyramid on his tongue,
    too-much-Holy-Spirit, too many ancestors

talking in a crowded room.
    My lover fears me:

    he only sees threat in my soil-
        brown eyes: a pending earthquake,

a possesion or a steep cliff, his imminent dive out of the closet.
        He fears the nature of my wild harvest,

the way I am hard fruit cracked open, soft
        inside, and his body drools.

He is not used to the howling woman on my tongue,
    not used to myth being truth.

Of course I'm a threat. My pulping heart is a caution
        sign, a red light he dare not cross because

he is not a man used to the elements,
    the ways of the Earth:

the way my love like fire ignites a forest;
        my pressence lifts him between

his thighs like wind does dust—

like sound bath or universe energy cascading onto
    cranium, jolting him into dance with me

past nirvana and all of God's children.
    He is a coward—a divide that swore

it would let me travel across its height without papeles.

My lover is a conditioned man since the start of time,
    a colonizer that fears the Pima Indian

    in me, the eagle, the flight, the ritual of me.
        He fears the too-bare earth-child, the savage,

the Tarahumara in me, fears the too bare human in me:
    the too masculine, female coalescence that makes me a god:

    the healer and warrior in me.

He tried to sever parts of me during his inner war:
    tried to slice me with his love like a molten silver sword.

He tried to fling my soft womb inflamed into abyss,
    but with my too-much-bidi-bidi-bom-bom in my hip,

    too-much-Frank-Ocean in my lovin',
        being too-much-divine and storm in the summer,

        being too good of a serpentine shapeshifter,
            I doged and shattered a fragile masculinity.

I, the two-spirit beast, am the reason why men build

walls, borders on their fingertips. I am the catalyst for why
    men don't shed tears, don't open up.

    To lovers I will always be a wild criatura, a danger, a disease,
        a howling spirit, a haunted house,

and God forbid I awake a man in our era of silence and crosses.
        Yet, although the man that swore he loved me left me runnin',

abandoned me, wings outstretched, crown in hand,
I hair-flipped knowing that silence

is the only way men will ever know how to love
because a freedom like me exists.

A Queer Girl's Ode to the Piragüero

Piragüero: a street vendor who serves traditional Puerto Rican ices

Oh, Piragüero! My first lover.
The only man I ever wanted
anything from. I sprinted half blocks
for you, got off the bus two stops early, took
the long way home, just to see
your rainbow umbrella.

Oh, Piragüero!
Candy-cool syrup god,
Boricua-batmobile,
wooden-cart-pushing-
bobsled papi.

When the viejitas ask for the tenth time
whether I got *un novio*,
the closest name on my tongue
was you! Who else made me break
my neck in two? Who else gave me so much
for a dollar? Who raised hell
when they nicknamed your island
delicacy *snow cone* (or worse) *shaved ice*?

I trusted you—the hallelujah work
of your bare hands, the dirty white kitchen towel
you laid over a fat block of ice &
never once did I ask questions.
& when they pushed you off
9th Ave., when you packed up
on 96th, I only saw you after ball games
on 131st & 5th; when the hipsters threw ice
in paper cups, added nutmeg & real ingredients like
mint leaves, called this an "upscale makeover"
for a poor man's treat, I wanted to shout out *No!*
Leave my man alone.

Tell me, who else
could turn a blue shopping cart
into a '57 Chevy? Or
a mom 'n' pop shop? Maybe the elotero
on El Centro, the churro ladies
by the A train. Maybe my mama, once
the nanny, who sowed curtains for a couple
upstairs, made an office out of her hands,
like my pops who
cut his saxophone into the velvet flesh
of night, rearranged the altitude
of a Palladium dance floor & then:
a plump wad of cash, a worn rubber band,
a 401(k) shoe box, which is to say
praise everything we build
under the table—the underworld
of workers & wielders,
America's thumping baseline,
the chorus of a country where
two-for-one is the best hook
to every good song
I know, like the way you
                        turn my tongue into
            a red carpet, like the first woman
I ever loved. Oh,

Piragüero. You winter
my whole mouth, you conductor
of cool; you're the only one
I know, the only one who can govern
the thick heat; like a DJ scratching
a glacier, you make
the whole city rock.

Eyes of an Outcast
After the art of Samira Abbassy

I am an outcast because I cast myself away from the liars,
the predators, the rapists, the molesters, the detesters of true
brilliance, and the fearful of the divine. And you, the
onlookers who examine us curiously as artifacts behind
delicate glass examined with confusion and dismissive
glances, you care not to go further than what meets the
naked I.

It is I behind the glass, shattered into a million particles of
stardust where nothing begins or ends.
You choose to misunderstand because it is easier that way.
Why dissect the truth when lies can be so pretty? Search no
further than the artificial, press us onto your skin like fake
tattoos so we can fade and you won't ever have to
remember that we existed at all.

Still we exist though you make us resist and break apart to
crumble, we glue ourselves together with art and grow like
a cancer in your conscience.
We watch ourselves grow and write biopsy poems,
malignant and benign, eradicating ourselves from your
radiating stares. You glare as if you knew who you were
before you became who you are.

You are a broken bone in a cast never to be truly mended.
You are the true outcast, not I, because in the wild I am
home and in your world I am a prisoner to your distorted
configurations of womanhood and reproductive stagnation.
I rebuke your blasphemy and locker-room fuckery. I was
once a lover who slept on featherbeds held by dandelion
petals, but now I am a peasant in your feudal system to be
pedaled.

If you could see through our Eyes and outcast the shadows,
we could find true depth even in the shallows. We could fly

with mended wings. We could let go of the sickness that clings and heal our wounds beneath a heaven that sings. We could cast out our nets and see what within it brings. We could jump on the diving board of life and offspring. You may cast me out but I can reel you in; you can cast your doubt but the truth will always win. You can place me in purgatory but I can forgive your sin. The overgrowth of wilderness will always help me to fit in.

Sonnet (the Mouth)

I have been so careless with the words I already have.
—Kaveh Akbar

1.
I don't want anyone
to tell me what I could have guessed—

that the mouth is a pit
for language.

2.
The mouth tenders
dialects like a mother

hen sits
on what it grows.

3.
I want to nestle the mouth
until it has done its clucking.

4.
For breakfast, I eat the mouth's
silent children

    & it feels like glue

on the pink roof of my palate. I dream
that my tongue has swelled

    & all my teeth are falling
out.

5.
I dream of two countries—

one grabs my hair
by the fistful,

    the other nibbles
    my toenails & waits

to bite.

6.
I dream of learning.
I want to learn
how people learn

to know
    when a boy is old enough

                to forget
his language,   when he is ready
                to be shredded.

7.
I know little of what shreds
a child into a man but think
one is best
        when he is begging.

I want to be both: a boy
& the woman he desires.

8.
I want to be the queerest
of kings

    to dribble down a jawline
    like rain. Maybe the mouth

is a lake. Maybe I have grown
in the mouth like a weed.

9.
When the mouth is gentle
    to me, one might see me dancing

244   in the low tide. Maybe I am ready
        to be plucked. Maybe the mouth

is a crater
     for the tongue.

10.
I forget the word for tongue
     in Spanish when a relative
asks me what I have bitten.

     Instead, I say *Mi boca es un cajón
lleno de cuchillos.* Everybody
     knows what I mean.

11.
By my age, my mother would have left
her country.

                    According to this measure
                    of courage, I am a coward

and ungrateful. My mother
says that she loves me

                    & calls me sharp-
                    tongued. I know what

my mouth can hold & it
is far too little. It juggles

                    words like a pocket might
                    with coins. Maybe language

is a currency. Maybe
language is power.

                    Maybe knowledge is stored
                    in the mouth.

12.
I do not know how to say my sexuality
in the language my mother was speaking
when she was my age
          so I coward
     my longing
            into English.

13.
All I want to know
is everything

that my mother
ever said.

14.
All I want
is to be a country

    where breath
    can stay

until ready to leave
the soft give

    of my wet
    & pink mouth.

preguntas frecuentes

en inglés el plural singular ya existe
el yo muchamente

en español tenemos que inventar el plural
ellx
    elle
un singular bastardo
    una caja de galletas /
duct tape /
unas esporsodas descompuestas/ en pegamento

en el idioma lo que ya existe no era
lo que será se da en el idiomx
en elle idioma
no importa el presente
tanto como el presente plural

¿cómo haces en español para existir
singularmente?
para mí es historia
entrenamiento para el presente
un bajar y subir de mi barbilla

en el inglich

    está la risa
ante el acento de bad bunny
que rechaza el no-acá del allá
de un español disfrazado de inglés
de la no-concordancia entre artículo y nombre

en español le decimos nombre
a la historia del tacto

pescamos mero que se come
los restos de los restos

comemos río
    bebemos arena
sufragamos los costos del sinfín

no es que no crea en líneas
por ejemplo

el círculo es una línea
que liga

un nudo es una línea cuir

en inglés
línea no tiene género

en español línea
es feminina dentro del idioma

un nudo

por ejemplo

en inglés el plural se hace singular
o al
singular
le da hambre de plural
o el plurisingular del inglés yo

o
dame la mano paloma
donde paloma es
rata aérea
o pacífica
o defecadora
suprema

o o
una mujer en un nido
pretexto para el canto

donde paloma es un nudo de distancias

248 entre techo y plaza
entre puente y piso
entre pie y suelo
un nudo de limitaciones

como lo somos

en idioma

no se trata
de si somos en uno
sino de si somos uno
si uno somos

¿entendéis?

en español el plural que nos
inventamos
suena a francés
a máquina de tiempo
que en cuerpo es para todos
whitman (jaja) en tu otoño
en vías de invierno metalúrgico
no hay hojas sino
hojas de hojalata
y pin plam cantamos el cuerpo
eléctrico con generador
en casos de emergencia

en español (en puerto rico)
inventar no se limita a crear objeto
sino a tramar encuentros

algo

y algo no se limita a cosa
se ata a inventar
vamos a inventar *algo*
por ejemplo

en el tiempo

que es jueves por la noche
nos inventamos un idioma
dentro de un idioma
dentro de un idioma
(una x dentro
de un puerto rico
dentro de un español)

en el trap
un género
    se inventa una canción
que contiene dos géneros (conejita y
conejo/pantalla y arete/uña y pintauña/
carne y costumbre)
que contiene un no lugar
del ahora (*qué se joda qué se joda*
qué se joda) que es también
el tramo histórico del olvido
en adición a cuántos cuatrenios
en los cuales se reinventa un apellido

una contradicción
es mal vista la mayoría de las veces
por ejemplo
ser del presente y a la vez denunciar un abuso

                pasado

tener antes y después de una tormenta
sin poner tormenteras
no decidirte por el género
ni denunciar la misoginia
que portas hoy y mañana
quizás saber lo absurdo del
dolor que causas

es mal visto

porque tampoco sabemos
conducir dentro de una casa
si es que isla es casa

250 si es que estadio es buen sitio
para ensayar juegos

los juegos seriamente
nos matan afuera

puedes dolerme
repentinamente memoriada
   el amor es así
familiar y excesivo

una contradicción es mal vista en ambos idiomas
a menos que le digas paradoja
que suena lindo y universitario

pero una contradicción es un nudo
línea que requeteliga

hasta que contestamos
no jodas

   vs. qué se joda

ambos usos de la idea de enredar
con un objeto puntiagudo

coser pero sin historia

línea pero sin garantías

un nudo es un nido de contradicciones
un género que se busca
y hiere el aire
un puño con puñal

   sonido
más sonido
pero diferente

ey
en vez de ay

e de indiferente
a la indiferencia
ala a del pájaro
de dos alas
   ala b
de la paloma

e siendo decadente
maraña

nudo nudo nudo
y ajenjo a sol
de luna

por ejemplo
en español
género es mi nombre
si le añado selectividad

también es una canción
y una contradicción si le quito
instrumento

uno no es uno
sino número y persona

substraer o añadir es mal visto
al menos que lo llames paradoja
que suena a universitario
arquitectura
o poema
por ejemplo

en inglichess
los poemas se comportan
muy bien si están a las malas
tienen porte

pero en español

252 (en puerto rico)
     (en uno)
     los poemas están en la mala
     la muy mala mala

     y salen muchas veces
     cantados

frequently asked questions

in english the singular plural already exists
the i manly

in spanish we have to invent the plural
ellx
    elle
a bastard singular
    a box of crackers /
duct tape /
soda decomposed / in glue

in language what already exists wasn't
what will be happens in languagx
in the(y) language
the present doesn't matter
as much as the plural present

how do you manage in spanish to exist
singularly?
for me it is history
training for the present
a going up and down my chin

in the inglich

    there is the laughter
at bad bunny's accent
which rejects the not-here of the there
of a spanish dressed as english
of the non-agreement between article and noun

in spanish we say name for noun
for the history of touch

we fish grouper or merefish
that eats the remains of remains

we eat river
    we drink sand
we defray the costs of the endless

it isn't that i don't believe in lines
for example

the circle is a line
that checks out

a knot is a queer line

in english
line has no gender

in spanish line
is feminine within language

a knot

for example

in english the plural becomes singular
or the
singular becomes hungry for plural
or the plurisingular of the english i

or
dame la mano paloma
or give me your hand pigeon
or give me your hand dove
or give me your hand paloma
where paloma is an aerial rat
or peaceful
or a supreme
defecator

or o or
a woman in a nest
who is pretext for song
where paloma is a knot of distances

between roof and plaza
between bridge and floor
between foot and ground
a knot of limitations

like we are

    in language

it isn't about
whether or not we are in one
but rather if we are one
if i one are

dost thou understand?

in spanish the plural we
    invent
sounds like french
a time machine
in the body is for all
whitman (jaja) in your autumn
on the way to metallurgic winter
there are no leaves only
leaves of tin
and pin plam we sing the body
electric with generator
in case of emergencies

in spanish (in puerto rico)
inventing isn't limited to creating objects
but rather to hatching encounters

    something

and something isn't limited to (some)thing
it is tied to inventing
let's invent *something*
for example

in time

which is thursday night
we invent a language
within a language
within a language
(an x within
a puerto rico
within a spanish)

in trap
a gen(d)re
    a song is invented
which contains two gen(d)res (bunnyette and
bunny / earring(screen) and earring / nail and nail polish /
flesh and custom)
that contains a no place
of now (*qué se joda qué se joda*
qué se joda) that is also
the historical stretch of oblivion
in addition to how many four-year terms
in which a last name is reinvented

a contradiction
has a bad rep most times
for example
to be of the present and at the same time denounce a past
    abuse
to have before and after a storm
without storm shutters
to not choose (decide-yourself) one gen(d)re
nor denounce the misogyny
you wear today and tmw
maybe knowing the absurdity of the
pain you cause

has a bad rep
because we also don't know
how to drive within a house
if an island is a house

if a stadium is a good place
to rehearse games

the games seriously
kill us outside

you can hurt (in me)
suddenly memoried
   love is like that
familiar and excessive

a contradiction has a bad rep in both languages
unless you call it paradox
which sounds pretty and very university

but a contradiction is a knot
line that superchecksout(something)

until we answer
fuck off

   vs. fuck it

both use the idea of entanglement
with a pointy object

to sew but without history

line with no guarantees

a knot is a nest of contradictions
a gen(d)re that seeks itself
and wounds the air
a fist with a knifeful

   sound
more sound
different

ey
instead of ay
or o or

e of indifferent(e)
to indifference
wing a of the bird
of two wings
    wing b
of the pigeon

e being decandent(e)
tangle

knot knot knot
and absinthe sun-soaked
by moon

for example
in spanish
gender is my name
if i add selectivity

it is also a song
and a contradiction if i take out
instrument

one is not one
but number and person

to add or subtract has a bad rep
unless you call it paradox
that sounds like university
architecture
or poem

for example

in inglichess
poems behave
very well if they are against well
they have poise

but in spanish
(in puerto rico)

(in one)
poems are in a bad way
the very bad bad

and they often come out
sung

A Letter from the X in Latinx

dear U,

> i've heard U don't know
>> how to say my name.
> i've heard U say
>> there's no way
>> to say it in spanish,
> i've heard U say
>> that it's a sound which doesn't exist,
> that it's an act
>> of imperialism by american
>> teenagers on the internet.

> i've heard U wanna know
>> my nation of origin

> just in case U need to protect
> spanish from me.

> i've heard U say:
>> we're not latin
> we don't speak latin
>> like you've never held a dollar
> or been to a funeral.

>> dimelo:
>> ¿que es la X en "mexica?"

> fake?
> i make that up too?
> shit, maybe i did.
> i know i made up my name,
> maybe i made up my whole history too.

> fuck it.
> sorry.

am I fucking up your language?
maybe i mean to.
maybe i mean to remind spanish that it's as uncomfortable on my tongue
as english, french, and latin before it.
maybe i mean to remind U this is nobody's country.
maybe i mean to remind U that we haven't heard the future yet,
maybe i do mean to fuck up your language

and your country
and your family
and your church

and your whole whack ass colonial gender system while i'm at it.

fuck it!
maybe i am an invention of the internet teens.
maybe i am a hallucination of the collective
        chingonxs who couldn't tell you when the mexican-american war
ended.

fuck it.
U don't know how to say my name?
good.
maybe i like it that way.
maybe i like a little uncertainty.

you don't know how to say my name?
here's one way:
like the x in mexica
"sh"
like latin-ish like only kinda latin,
or like: latineshhh
like latine-shhhhh like be quiet
or the grammar police will ask where we came from.

here's another: latinx, rhymes with ese,
Phonetically, in spanglish, "X" = "eje" = "eh? hey!"
as in eh? hey! you tried to leave without paying

respect!

i've heard U've got a lot of questions
and don't like digging for answers.
i've heard U don't like how
history feels under fingernails.
i've heard U ask how to say my name.

U do it with respect.

besos,
la X en latinx

See

see my father's mother | tongue lodged in my throat
quetzal preening | round my rib cage

see my Coke-bottle cock | queer as can be
but still be | on brand

see my tangle | of arteries
like vines | cling to sinew

see my hands as light | as clouds
that carry | rain&rain&rain

& see my body | ascend upper
rings | of sight&sight&sight

my body a blur | red periphery
| slow | ly be | coming
                                                    | clear.

Where I Inherit My Silence

i once walked into
my grandfather's shadow

dug for spanish
with a stick of dynamite

felt it explode
on my mother tongue

i bruised
& he called them flowers

i spoke english
& he fed me more spanish

until my stomach knew
the taste of vinegar

how his gold ring whistled
me to sit & stay

& i became
a puddle of mud

i split myself in half
like any good exorcist

accent marks left me
like a startled bird

& i have yet
to speak honey

i carry pieces
of a tambourine

Found Fragment on Ambition

5.
if a hood is a sense of place
& a sense of place is identity
then identity is a hood & adult /
hood is being insecure in any
hood a hood scares the whitest
folks why folks scared to stop
in the hood & why folks stop
wearing a hood & call it white
nationalism if i tried i would
fail to pass if i failed i would
try to pass when can i retire my
bowl stop needing to beg for my
personhood you see academically
my ghetto pass was revoked please
sir can you direct me to the window
to turn in my man card where
can i apply to enter the whiteness
protection program i've lost
my found identity is a hood
a hood is a sense of place
a place places a hood hood in us

Julian Randall

On the Night I Consider Coming Out to My Parents

I am afraid, of something I am, but have never named. My tongue is a refuge for secrets. How does one still fear banishment if they were born an exile? There's blood on the ground; no time remains so I'll lay it flat: I am Black and Dominican and Bisexual. There. If I die now, you'll have a hint for which god to petition. Sometimes, I look at a man and my hands are already digging into the small country of his back. In this way, the body is a distraction from what can make the body just a memory. My lips could bring a man's blood to the surface; my mother raised a curse and gave it her face. I am afraid to belong to another thing, to become still more no-man's-land. I am a trench; nobody comes to clear the dead. Somewhere, my mother is gripping a rosary to pray for men who look like me. Somewhere, my mother is praying for me. I do not want to give her something else to worry about. I am quiet, I bury no one, blood is drying beneath my nails. I do not know which me it belongs to.

Night Plays My (Father's) Song After the Azealia Banks Concert

A slow malice dedicated to the unmasking.

Nail polish next to the bejeweled, sunlit.

Now who is who, is transition.

Thin white cloth, prayer for touch with the Goddess of a darling ego.

Pero it was never about you, just a boy with a green bottle perched on his lips

asking me if this was what I wanted.

/

Shallow linens fall about me.

I choose fluorescence, surrounded by queer men looking so hungry for—

Papi said *I never drank when I danced or if I did I would sweat the liquor*

onto the walls.

My father hungered for himself; I hunger for someone to consume me.

/

No one kisses you because you don't know your own lips, just wear them out at
   night.

What disappears es desaparecido in any clothing.

You sink into the breath of night, you are only an echo.

/

If I wanted joy   I didn't
If I wanted his body   I wouldn't
dare sink so toothless into milk.

On Confessionalism

Not sleepwalking, but waking still,
 with my hand on a gun, and the gun
in a mouth, and the mouth
 on the face of a man on his knees.
Autumn of '89, and I'm standing
 in a section 8 apartment parking lot,
pistol cocked, and staring down
 at this man, then up into the mug
of an old woman staring, watering
 the single sad flower to the left
of her stoop, the flower also staring,
 my engine idling behind me, a slow
moaning bassline and the bark
 of a dead rapper nudging me on.
All to say, someone's brokenhearted.
 And this man with the gun in his mouth—
this man who, like me, is really little
 more than a boy—may or may not
have something to do with it.
 May or may not have said a thing
or two, betrayed a secret, say,
 that walked my love away. And why
not say it: she adored me. And I,
 her. More than anyone, anything
in life, up to then, and then still,
 for two decades after. And, therefore,
went for broke. Blacked out and woke
 having gutted my piggy and pawned
all my gold to buy what a homeboy
 said was a beretta. Blacked out
and woke, my hand on a gun, the gun
 in a mouth, a man, who was really
a boy, on his knees. And because
 I loved the girl, I actually paused
before I pulled the trigger—once,
 twice, three times—then panicked

not just because the gun jammed,
　　but because what if it hadn't,
because who did I almost become,
　　there, that afternoon, in a section 8
apartment parking lot, pistol cocked,
　　with the sad flower staring, because
I knew the girl I loved—no matter
　　how this all played out—would never
have me back. Day of damaged ammo,
　　or grime that clogged the chamber.
Day of faulty rods, or springs come
　　loose in my fist. Day nobody died,
so why not *hallelujah*? Say *amen* or
　　thank you? My mother sang for years
of God, babes, and fools. My father,
　　lymph node masses fading from
his x-rays, said surviving one thing
　　means another comes and kills you.
He's dead, and so, I trust him. Dead,
　　and so I'd wonder, years, about the work
I left undone—boy on his knees
　　a man now, risen, and likely plotting
his long way back to me. Fuck it.
　　I tucked my tool like the movie gangsters
do, and jumped back in my bucket.
　　Cold enough day to make a young man
weep, afternoon when everything,
　　or nothing, changed forever. The dead
rapper grunted, the bassline faded,
　　my spirits whispered something
from the trees. I left, then lost the pistol
　　in a storm drain, somewhere between
that life and this. Left the pistol in
　　a storm drain, but never got around
to wiping away the prints.

Gang Relations

In middle school,
some friends and I
started a "gang"
called "Mexicans
Tear Shit Up,"
or *MTSU*.
A subterfuge,
joke, dumb parody
to those who knew
our dads would die laughing
or whip asses
if our game came into view.

To the square, the shy,
the provincially "white,"
we served fear on a platter
and, smiling wildly,
fed them small bites.

Sharpie pens proclaimed
our (play)set
on the backs of bus seats,
under textbook covers,
on desktops.
MTSU, foo!
What, foo?!
What?! What?!!

Feigned violence
counted for humor
and marked the edge
of our toughness.

Then, a crew of cousins
moved from LA
to get away

from the bang,
la jura,
the drug game trap.
They drew earnest Xs
through our sarcastic tags.
When fate placed us
(smiling) face
to (crying-smiling) face,
with squinting eyes and jaws
jabbing, they claimed:
Ghost town, ey!
Ghost town!
Where you from, ey?!
as their fingers splayed
into menacing shapes.

My friends and I
didn't know what to say,
but we knew to turn,
walk the other way.

MTSU died that day.
We never spoke of it again.
Neither did they.

Did You Hear What They Said?
After Gil Scott-Heron

for Nestora Salgado & for those who fast

They said another mother's dead,
dead and can't be buried. Forty-three children
disappeared after capture. Another mother
cries for half a millennium in the desert
searching for her daughter's daughter
(the deserts of our country, the only crop
remaining). Hear what the mothers are saying.
They are Constitution bound. They are found
as the many remains in a waste, an arroyo.
Fill the heart with what another mother
is saying. Rise up in unison, a voice
for the chorus of peace. Another wave
is added to the saving waters. Here,
in Anahuac, the Place Between Two Great
Waters, all of the unburied join in. Feast,
sing between the weeping. Did you hear
what they are saying? Women and children first.

My Father's Blasphemy (or Excerpts from Shit My Puerto Rican Father Says)

*

It is music that spits in the face of the church, adding shit, whores, leaven bread, and classic f-bombs. We know it better than any scripture. My sisters, brother, and I quote him with the same pauses and emphasis that taught us you can't always hold compassion in your heart. Sometimes you need to tell the insurance agent, who just raised your premiums, "I might be a little man, but I'll stomp your ass all over this parking lot."

*

My father's version of "the talk" happens when I am seventeen. I'm driving, and I remember the stretch of Cheyenne Mountain Road just before the movie theater and shopping center. He turns and asks, "Do you know about sex?" I answer, "Yes." He concludes the conversation with, "Good. Don't do it." He changes the subject back to silence, leaving me with what I need to know.

*

When my dad's knee swells up from the embedded grenade shrapnel from Korea, mom won't let him mow the lawn. He argues his case: "The doctor don't give a shit if I cut the grass or if I set it on fire." The compromise is him supervising, me mowing, and her watching him not mow. Whenever she goes inside, he takes the mower away to cut a row of grass before giving it back to me. I try to cover for him by mimicking his style and form.

*

On vacation, we order breakfast at a mom-and-pop restaurant in Ecuador. Dad helps the time pass with his irritation: "Now we need to wait for them to finish milking the goddamn cow." A little later, he adds, "They caught the chicken and now they're shaking out the eggs." At the end of the meal, just like he does at every other restaurant, he smacks his lips in satisfaction and declares, "Not bad."

*

During a visit home, father asks me if I want a Puerto Rican omelet. Of course, I ask what is a Puerto Rican omelet, and he answers, "What the hell else am I supposed to call it when a Puerto Rican makes you an omelet?" He makes the omelet with two types of cheese, ham, bell peppers, tomato, and a side of arroz. A little later, he asks my niece if she wants a Puerto Rican omelet.

*

Every time I call my parents, I ease into speaking Spanish with my mom for awhile. I get comfortable, she teaches me words I don't know, and she corrects when I stumble. When she passes the phone to my father, he greets me with, "What's up, Papo?" and calls me baby and talks to me in English. I ask him about how he's feeling. He always answers, "I'm cool, baby. I'm cool."

Pastoral

The cows chewing on the field-grass have only
a partial belief in god. They believe in god the way
I believe in my own goodness. The flies

that hang around their asses disperse
when the cows flinch, and gather again.
I've been told terrible things about the impact

of my words. I try to use them more carefully
as I grow older. Some young people look up to me
now that I only ridicule others to myself.

It's hard not to admire the tranquility of these cows
that buckle their legs beneath the shade of ash trees
while listening to the distant snaps of machinery

invented to ease the slaughter. I was young.
I may still be. I hurt people that I loved, and I believed
in forgiveness as one of the many laws of nature

on my side.

Rules at the Juan Marcos Huelga School (Even the Unspoken Ones)

This should be posted in every classroom until the end of the school year:

1) No more than one child
out of the classroom at one time.

[*They might run away, a monarch
butterfly tugged in the direction of
the wind.*]

2) The upstairs classes will not make
excess noise because there are no walls
between classes and
the noise carries downstairs too.

[*Noise that needs to be made should
flame out in a bonfire, out on the
roof, where sunlight can hear it all.*]

3) Any mothers coming
into the classroom—send them
to the principal's office, unless
they are teachers' helpers.

[*They need to go, to help the
principal birth a school that can
speak and spell the words
revolución, and work, and hands,
and huelga.*]

4) No running
in the hallways or stairways.

[*Wait for nighttime, children,
when you can run and race around
in the dark, in the cool of the trees,
yelling that you caught a star on the tip
of your tongue; then you realize; you
ran around 'til morning and it is the
dew on the tips of tree leaves you
taste.*]

5) No screaming or shouting
in the classrooms,
hallways, or stairways.

[*Shout on paper, written boldly,
in a book, in the middle of an open
field, in the street, in the classroom,
make sure your voice shrills.*]

6) No throwing of paper
or trash on the floor.

[*In my class, I will teach you
to throw Molotov cocktails, bright
orange ones, that whistle in the air,*]

and when they smash on those crazy
school laws, they will burst in a
bright yellow the scent of lemon,
burnt wood that will take over for
a few days.]

7) No one can go to Poppa Burger.

[*In the future, the streets are still*
the same, and in December, on a
Tuesday afternoon in 2016, one of
your decedants will be stabbed
merely for standing in the day.
The Northside knows scar, knows
body, when it needs to mourn.]

8) If you take your class to the park,
be sure that everyone crosses
the street,
going and coming.

[*Move in packs, march the streets*
together, keep the body flickering,
make the voice resist quiet, this
going, this coming, is resistance.]

9) All shirts will be buttoned.

[*This is how we mean business:*
you come to school, bien fino,
and we will teach you the four
winds, the reason we are always
armed to the touch of a blade; we
are always blades, bien filoso.]

10) Be sure that your classroom is
reasonably clean before you let
the class out at the end of the day.

[*One day all these classrooms*
will no longer hold any of us,
leave no evidence we were here,
we exist in the whisper,
the tender cinnamon strings in
muscle. Marcha ya.]

Villa Blanca Affair

Mamí raised me,
papí gave me his name
being a married
father of three,
two boys, same name as he,
Orlando Flores.

Product of
absent gardner,
I've never been
fan of flowers!
too close to the smell
of funeral service.

Death no longer
makes me nervous,
like when I was young,
woke up screaming,
"I don't want to die"
after realizing

the curse of mortality;
identity
was a burden
left unspoken,
and I spoke silence fluently—
so did papí.

Maybe I'm depravity,
lost evidence
remembrance of
Villa Blanca affair
dare I say?

I've buried
what resembles him most,

to escape
fatherless ghost
each time
resurrected to a name,

any name
but the name of;
forgotten, absent,
abandoned, left behind
reminds me how trauma
causes dissociation often!

Papí does not know
his lineage is coffin,
call me Grim Reaper!

my seed
will not be keepers
of that name,
will not bear

el apellido
de su Abuelo,
will not follow
tradition.

We know the power
of decision!
Call me
misplaced conviction!

Say it's spite,
in spite of affliction,
aberration,
of patriarchal system.

You must think
you some kind of God
planting yourself
all abroad

282   just to say
        you can find forever!

If you ever address me

call me
Mamí's maiden name,
child support
you lied not to pay,

call me
like you never called me
knowing my number.

Remember I said:
"nobody saved me
when I called on you the most,"
you cried, I didn't.

Knowing all
the reasons why
Te Amo
never rose
out of your mouth.

Valuable lesson,
no doubt!
To learn
not to be like you.

I go back home
and always find you

to make sure
you know
I'll never forget
who raised me.

Auténtico

Instead of writing poetry about my dad, I burned sage and I prayed, which is new for me.

Instead of writing poetry about my dad, I drank two shots of tequila at my desk, which isn't new for me.

Instead of writing poetry about my dad, I slept until noon.

Instead of writing poetry about my dad, I thought about: US nationalism and the death of John McCain, the language of police scanners, my complicity with Mexican hegemony, my inability to focus while at work, the friends I no longer speak to, my next paycheck, the way my anxiety feels in my chest (like a loaded spring), and the selfishness of my future, in no order whatsoever. And I also thought about: the wall that exists invisibly between me and both of my parents.

Instead of writing poetry about my dad, I made myself think about anything else.

Instead of writing poetry about my dad, I enjoyed a memory. In the memory, I am drunk in Spain singing Kesha songs loud in the street with the friends from college that I no longer speak to. Instead of writing poetry about my dad, I thought about writing each of these friends a letter. Yes, I thought. I would make these letters as beautiful and honest and urgent as I could write them. But instead of writing poetry about my dad or letters to these friends, I had a second memory, which I didn't enjoy. In this memory, I'm with my mom in the car parked outside the bank, and she is crying. We'd been fighting about something unimportant, and I corrected her use of a word. She tells me I make her feel stupid. Later, my dad will tell me something very similar. He'll tell me: *Son, it isn't what you say, it's how you say it. If you give me food on a trash can lid, I won't eat it. Put it on a plate.*

Instead of writing poetry about my dad, I thought about: how I've come to say things. About the languages I gained at the expense of others. About why I write for other people these days (or don't, at all) instead of calling home. About why I didn't explain any of this to my mom the day I made her cry.

Instead, I apologized to her, I said: I didn't mean it like that. And I thought about the distances separating me from her, from both of them. I thought about how time and language and education and America had built (yes) a wall invisibly between us, and I wondered if we'd ever understand each other again. I thought about how I never wanted to be the kind of son who corrects his parents. I didn't tell her any of this. I still haven't told her this, not really. I was about to, earlier today, but then, instead, I thought about something else.

Instead, I thought about the first time I saw my dad cry. This was only last week— in the twenty-eight years leading up to that night, I had never seen him cry. And I never expected it to shake me as much as it did, but it did. I remember thinking about the kind of pressure it must have taken to make him crack. I remember feeling like I caught a glimpse of his real, authentic self. And it shook me to learn some real things about him. Except, no. What did I learn about him, actually? Not much. As usual, he didn't actually say a whole lot that night. But what he did say was enough that filling in the gaps between his words is still terrifying me.

Instead of writing poetry about my dad, I thought about him, and my mom, and that wall between us. I thought about the day she cried, and why she did. I thought about how I say what I say. I thought about that night he cried, and why he did. How he says what he says. I thought about: the way his voice morphed into someone else's, how it sounded like mine, how he said some things he probably never said to anyone before in his life, except maybe my mom—in that exact order. I thought about coping, and not coping. And speaking and not speaking. I thought about the patterns of my dad's speech. His circular way of talking. I thought about how whenever he gives one of his speeches, whenever he offers this or that advice to us, he usually comes back to the same few platitudes that don't really say anything at all. He says them over and over again, and I thought about: why that is so unspeakably important. I thought about: the way my mom understands him. I thought about my dad, carving the marrow out of a language he had to teach himself, and crawling inside. I thought about metaphors, especially the ones that don't really say anything at all, like: *a wall between me and my parents*, or *a wall of silence*, or *a wall of emptiness*, or *a wall of never-ending generational misunderstanding*. Or even: *a bridge*. I thought about something, anything, that could mean more than that. Like putting food on a plate. I thought about everything I couldn't say to him the night I saw him cry and heard him speak in another way, and all the things he couldn't say back to me.

Instead of writing poetry about my dad, I tried anything. I tried tequila, I tried sage. I tried writing letters. Instead of writing poetry about my dad, I almost did. I came so close.

The Lion-Head Belt Buckle

My father bought it for me as a gift in the Madrid *rastro*
near where we lived, new immigrants from Cuba.

The eyes and mane carved deep into the metal, the tip of the nose
already thin with the blush of wear. My mother found a brown

leather strap and made it into a belt with enough slack and holes
to see me wearing it in Los Angeles where we landed next.

My father worked at *Los Dos Toros*, a meat market run by Papito,
a heavey-set man with a quick smile, and when I would visit

the market after school to wait for my father to bring me home,
Papito always talked to me about baseball and his favorite

Cincinnati Reds players. It was there one of his employees,
a skinny man with deep-set eyes and crow-feather-black

hair would stop me in the narrow hallway by the produce tables
and grab the belt buckle and praise it. All along passing his hand

over my penis. "You are strong," he would whisper, "like this lion."
I would recoil from his touch and move away back to the front

where Papito would ask me about what bases I intended
to play next season on *Los Cubanitos* team. I never told my father,

or anyone, but the afternoon I showed up and the Fire Department
and police and ambulances huddled in the alleyway behind

Los Dos Toros, I knew something terrible had happened. Some
other kid had uttered the man's groping and insistence on a kiss

in the *almacén,* the darkened storage room past the meat locker.
And another father had taken matters into his own hands.

286   But instead I found my father hosing the backdoor entrance,
       washing the blood down to the alleyway. He told me to wait for him

       in the car. The paramedics rolled out Papito, shot and dead on a stretcher,
       victim of a holdup. The dark Cuban man who'd felt me up time

       and again stood in the shade of a tree weeping and kicking the dirt
       with blood-encrusted shoes. I found out later he was the one who

       slammed the assailant against the wall and beat him unconscious.
       Fuerte como un leon. The words fluttered like cowbirds in the back

       of my mind. Scattershot and ringing like the violence among the men.

Endomorph (n.)

Human physical type (somatotype) tending toward roundness, as determined by the physique-classification system developed by American psychologist W. H. Sheldon. The extreme endomorph has a body as nearly globular as humanly possible. He has a round head, a large, round abdomen, large internal organs relative to his size, rather short arms and legs with fat upper arms and thighs, but slender wrists and ankles. The endomorph body type is solid and generally soft. Endomorphs gain fat very easily. Under normal conditions, the endomorphic individual has a great deal of body fat, but he is not simply a fat person. If starved, he remains an endomorph.

endomorphic (adj.)

1. of or pertaining to, the endomorph, possessing the qualities of the somatotype.
Karen normally didn't date endomorphic dudes, but he was funny, so she made an exception.

2. of, or pertaining to, the fat boy's tentative kiss in his car the night he took her to TGI Friday's.
Karen pitied his endormorphic kiss, especially when she told him to stop building things up in his head.

3. of, or pertaining to, the ritual mistaking of love for mercy.
Karen said that his endomorphic desires led her to question her sexuality.

4. of, or pertaining to, the lights out before sex.
Karen flipped an endomorphic light switch and was shocked to discover that fat boys be fucking for keeps.

5. of, or pertaining to, the shock of discovering that fat boys be fucking for keeps.
Karen decided to ignore the endomorphic manner of her surprised breath, and concentrate instead on her quiver, her sudden, how soft his lips were.

endomorph (v.)

Look folks. I think he lost some weight. Look. Doesn't he look sleeker today than yesterday? Look. He's slimmer from the day I met him. Look. He's so much better now. Look. He's losing weight. Seriously. Look. No really, stop and look. That's my sleek baby. Tell me he hasn't lost weight. Look. He is doing so good now. Isn't he doing so good?

Man, look. All I ever do is cook vegetarian for him. He should be grateful. He better be, shit. The way they stare at us. It's the least he could do. Of course, he likes it. He tells me all the time.

endomorph (v. irregular)

1. To sit naked and stare at the marvelous gravity that created the beast in my mirrors.

2. To contemplate the mixture of oils and American petrochemical residue combining inside my skin to compose the minor chord.

3. The airplane does not feature me.

4. The bus refuses my advances.

5. The elevator door opens. Ten people shift nervously. Laugh, they relax. I wait for the next one, the next one, the next.

6. Look for a dent in the guardrail shaped like my car.

7. Because this is the embankment I chose.

8. Your children tug your shirt and ask why is that man so fat, mommy. You hush them, quickly.

9. I like you, but I understand this is not a date.

10. I turn the lights off before you fuck me. You say thank you.

If Anybody's Interested

Authorities' got hands on their sticks
Ready and quick to pull out the proverbial whip
And a glock full of clips
While we're driving in our whip
Cops are on their way to market
While we're the ones unarmed
Not believing we are the target
Not recalling that to them
We're just another Trayvon Martin
Sean Bell and Eric Garner
Human beings being murdered

Whatever happened to "Serve and Protect"
They break civilian necks and get a slap on the wrist
Un-policed police mostly get away with it
I trust police the way I trust the government
In God we trust to see some punishment
We know the system is corrupted
Sometimes they get sentenced for their injustices
But most times they whistle by
Acting like they did none of it

There's a long list of names spoken over walls of silence
In a world of violence, the tyrants don't get tired
Our brains are rewired to follow roads to nowhere
People growing scared calling life unfair
Complacent like they don't care, afraid to make a statement
I declare don't be another slave on the plantation
Divided segregation, displaced like first nations
Suicide statistics are high in elevation
We're forced on reservations
Modern gentrification
Drug and liquor integration
Militarization
Sex sells on every station
It's a third-eye invasion

Terrorist interrogation
Modern-day enslavement
The color of your skin is under investigation
Racial condemnation
Ego inflation, superiority-complex implementation
Stop-and-frisk statistics are rising for the innocent
But if you aren't interested, don't listen to this gibberish
Forget the politrix of this matrix that we're living in
It's all part of the system and it's always going to be like
This
If you aren't questioning the roots of white privilege

Lady Fine Is for Sugar

My grandmother believed in it
delicate laugh perfectly pressed blouse
blouse not shirt and proper grammar
billowing it out

You are well, not fine. Fine is for sugar!

Shorthand typing secretarial position
with some florid-faced boss drew success
my mother stormed like rain
teen pregnancy loud laugh bellicose
swore freely in front of her children

i am the sky that could fall either way

Lady passé and enduring mythology
i feel some sorta way over Cardi B
precisely because she levitated up her stripper pole
like a fuckin' phoenix against the stench
of respectability politics

like a motherfuckin' phoenix through the ceiling
burning on the hydrogen of unwavering respect
bricks of dollar signs gain you
plush in the same country where abuela believed
you had to play the Lady game

Star-spangled fantasy
my mother knew the danger
the voice that can't be heard
the suspect testimony of that pressed blouse
flesh-tone foundation obscures
black and blues
white peter pan collar
crossed ankles
the *I'm well thank you.*

Brown Girl in Therapy
After Ebony Isis Booth

When you leave therapy in tears, once again, driving 95 mph /
down the I-25 for the second or fiftieth time / you begin to question
if your hard- / fought-for, expensive-as-all-hell / insurance is worth
the trauma / because you can't remember, not even one time /
you felt any better because therapy taught you to smile / and all
you know / is that you are driving too fast / for salt-soaked blurred vision /
and she is blonde and blue-eyed / and the lead intake psych- /
chologist told you, that she is a good fit for you / but you know it is only
because she is a woman / and that is all he sees / and she is at least fifteen
years your junior / her eyes are so damn blue / blue and clear and wide-
eyed and innocent / nothing like your own / then you feel / sorry /
for her / talking of blood and crack / and how Compton broke your
father and this is why he is cold / nevermind the time mom's nose
was smacked wide open with his palm / and you were
only baby-soft and ten years old / so you cry when you don't want to /
and she nods and passes you a tissue box / you notice it is not a generic /
brand and wish it were / because at least you would feel a bit more at home /
at the sight of discounted accoutrements that remind you / of a home
that never really was / a home / in the very least / so, you pay the damn bill
that comes in the mail two weeks later / vow to never return / never to drive
95 mph with salt-stained eyes again / instead write a poem you never /
nevernevernevernever want to publish / anyways / and don't go back
to therapy / that's for damn sure / even though she has framed
her scrolled diplomas and hung them / on the wall / and they remind you of little
sheets of curled flesh / and this is because only white
girls / relate to that type of bullshit / and in the end that is all
that it ever was / anyways / bullshit / and no one ever told her / that Brown
girls love / their pain more than they love themselves.

Queer Joy Mijx

tongue kissing gender in front
of the family taquero

abrázando mi carne
a warm tortilla de maiz

Abuelita following the line
of my skin fade

to Mexico, shots of patrón
i'm grown, un sol tremendo

tías singing
por tu maldito amor

to the abandoned lazy boys
of my tíos

carrying Garcia
thru borders of body

parakeet in the cage
pretty bird, pretty bird

smile @ me from the window
of the kitchen

i am still
in the backyard

w/ a plate full
of barbacoa

waiting for you
to bring me a fork

Hasta la Madre

for Susana

south
of lines drawn in useless places
a generation abandoned by men too caged to feel
screams
estamos hasta la madre.

north of those lines
they say fatherless.
south of,
we say motherful,

we say
hasta la madre

also meaning *we are fed up*

but if you listen to the hasta one more time
do you hear how
the fed (up) become the nurtured,
and we amen to the women who raised us?

Rain

the first time I ask Tana why she left El Salvador,
me dice: *porque allá llueve mucho.* its waters too vast and devious,
too quick to wash away everything she's worked for.

for weeks, Tana watched horizon fall to earth
from bus windows. she held on tightly
to herself, and the thought of mi mami, su hija,
borders away and alone somewhere in the capital.

no hay tiempo para esas babosadas, she thought
wiping her eye-made rain away.
she massaged her bloody feet into silence,
her throat aching for just one sip.

//
for years, I am afraid of rain.
I am six years old and praying for sun.
when rainfall begins, I run
indoors, am caught somewhere
by my elementary school teacher
in a cafeteria corner, crying.
I am six years old and believe
every time it rains, it is time to flee.
I am six years old and afraid
of being left behind.
I am six years old and my blood remembers
what it feels to leave
a whole homeland behind.

//
a Salvadoran woman once wrote that
our poetry has never had the luxury of being enamored with the moon.
perhaps this is why all my poems are about the sun,
about coming from women who have survived by chasing it,
women who go only where the light will feed them,
women who leave the second they suspect a flood.

Acknowledgments

Angélica Maria Aguilera   "The Red Dress" first appeared in Angélica Maria's self-published chapbook *Body Flag*.

Amanda Alcántara   "Nunca seré fina" was first published in *Chula*.

Diannely Antigua   "Immigration Story" and "In the Country Where My Parents Met in a Taxicab" were previously published in *Ugly Music*. "Immigration Story" was first published in *Tinderbox Poetry*.

José Angel Araguz   "La Llorona Watches the Movie *Troy*" was previously published in the poetry collection *Small Fires*.

William Archila   "Advice to a Migrant Collecting Dead Things Ever Since He Learned the Length of Walking" was first published in *Missouri Review*.

Sara Borjas   "Míja" was first published in *Shot Glass*. "Mexican Bingo" was first published in *McNeese Review*.

Andrés Cerpa   "Portrait and Shadow" was originally published by *Kenyon Review*. "Seasonal Without Spring: Summer" was originally published by *Gulf Coast*. Both poems are included in the debut collection *Bicycle in a Ransacked City: An Elegy*.

Victoria Chávez Peralta   "When Collin Chanted 'Build the Wall'" was published in *Columbia Poetry Review*.

Alan Chazaro   "Ode to Kendrick Lamar" originally appeared in *Public Pool*. "Broken Sestina as Soundscape" originally appeared in *Minnesota Review*. Both poems are forthcoming in *Piñata Theory*.

Davon Clark — "Pantoum for Puerto Rico" was first published in *Line Break Chicago Zine, Vol. 1* and digitally at *Button Poetry*.

Bailey Alejandro Cohen-Vera — "Sonnet (The Mouth)" was first published in *Muzzle Magazine*.

Karla Cordero — "Where I Inherit My Silence" and "Leaked Audio from a Detention Center" were first published by [*PANK*] in its folio, *LATINX: LATINIDAD*.

Gabriel Cortez — "Fat Joe At The Ninth Grade Dance" was first published in *The Rumpus*.

Carina del Valle Schorske — "Friend, This Is What Hurts" was first published as part of *Gulf Coast*'s 2016 portfolio of Marigloria Palma's work.

Jaquira Díaz — "December" was first published in *Salon*.

Stefanie Clara Fernández — "Notes from the Valley of a Hundred Fires" was first published in *Yale Daily News* magazine.

Ariel Francisco — "Eating Dinner Alone at the 163rd Street Mall" was first published in *Scalawag Magazine* and is forthcoming in the book *A Sinking Ship is Still a Ship*. "In Response to People Trying to Rename the South Bronx 'The Piano District'" was previously published in *Breakwater Review* and *All My Heroes Are Broke*.

Malcolm Friend — "Failed Bomba" and "Ode to Tego Calderón (or The Day *El abayarde* Dropped Was Maelo's Resurrection)" previously appeared in *Our Bruises Kept Singing Purple*.

Denice Frohman — "Doña Teresa & the Chicken" was first published in *Adroit Journal*. "A Queer Girl's Ode to the Piragüero" was originally published in *Acentos Review*.

Benjamin Garcia	"The Language in Question" first appeared in *Puerto del Sol,* and "Ode to the Peacock" first appeared in *New England Review.*
Suzi F. Garcia	A version of "The Bridge Is Out" was originally published in *Anthropoid.*
Carlos Andrés Gómez	"Hijito" was published in *Backbone Press*, and "Before the Last Shot" was first published in *Solstice Literary Magazine* and subsequently *Sequestrum Literary Journal* as winner of the 2018 Sequestrum Editor's Reprint Award in Poetry.
Mariana Goycoechea	An earlier version of "PoEma for MaMi" was first published in *Acentos Review.*
Isa Guzman	"Títere Ring" was first published in the anthology *Birds Fall Silent in the Mechanical Sea*, published by Great Weather for Media.
Leticia Hernández-Linares	"Her Arms Filled with Stars" was first published in [PANK].
Grecia Huesca Dominguez	"Mexican Remedies" was first published by *Acentos Review.*
Karl Michael Iglesias	"Tonight's Blackout" was originally published in *Acentos Review.*
Antonio Lopez	"Apology to Her Majesty, Queen Cardi B" was first published in *Lunch Ticket.*
Sheila Maldonado	"infinite wop" was previously published online at *Gulf Coast.*
Nancy Mercado	"First Mourning" was first published in *Fifth Wednesday.*
Samuel Miranda	"We Is" is included in the poetry collection *We Is* and was first published in *Acentos Review.*

John Murillo	"On Confessionalism" was first published in *The Common*. "Poem Ending and Beginning on Lines by Larry Levis" first appeared in *jubilat*.
Mauricio Novoa	"Dandelion Graves" was first published in *The Wandering Song: Central American Writing in the United States*, and "Jailhouse Library" first appeared in *Acentos Review*.
Javier Perez	"Amaizeing Grace" was first published in *Acentos Review*.
Janel Pineda	"In Another Life" was previously published in *Wildness* by Platypus Press.
Ana Portnoy Brimmer	"Patria" was first published in *Revista Trasunto*; "Home" is forthcoming in the chapbook *To Love an Island*, winner of the 2019 Vinyl 45 Chapbook Contest by YesYes Books.
Reyes Ramirez	"Eddie Guerrero Enters a Ring Holding the World Championship" was first published in *December Magazine*.
Julian Randall	"Translation" was first published in *New York Times* magazine. "On the Night I Consider Coming Out to My Parents" first appeared in *Callaloo*. Both are included in the collection *Refuse*.
Monica Rico	"Soy de la Luna / I Am from the Moon (Volveré a la Luna / I Will Return to the Moon)" was previously published in *Glass: A Journal of Poetry (Poets Resist)*. "Poem in Consideration of My Death" was first published in *Cosmonauts Avenue*.
Joseph Rios	"Fellowship Application" first appeared in *Normal School*. "Round Two: Saving Nations" appeared in *Shadowboxing: Poems and Impersonations*.

Peggy Robles Alvarado

"My Spanglish" was first published in *Latinas: Voices of Protest and Struggles in Twenty-First-Century USA.*

Raquel Salas Rivera

"preguntas frecuentes / frequently asked questions" was first published in *Small Axe Salon* and later as an independent "poema suelto" by *La Impresora.*

Jani Rose

"What's in a Name" was first published in *Acentos Review.*

MJ Santiago

"Self-Portrait as My Ancestry, la Malinche" was previously published by *The Shallow Ends*, and an earlier version of "More Than One but Less Than Any" was published by *No, Dear* magazine.

Nicole Sealey

"And" previously appeared in *New Sound.* "An Apology for Trashing Magazines in Which You Appear" appeared in *Best New Poets 2011.*

Christopher Soto

"[Somewhere in Los Angeles] This Poem Is Needed" was first published in *American Poetry Review.*

Vincent Toro

"On Bombing" was first published in *BOAAT.* "First Voice: DREAMcatcher" and "Second Voice: Sleep Dealer (dir. Alex Rivera)" were first published in *Chiricú Journal: Latina/o Literatures, Arts, and Cultures.*

Sydney Valerio

"Chivo Liniero" was written for Valerio's one-woman show *Matters* and was first published in print in La Pluma y La Tinta's 2018 *New Voices Anthology.*

Javier Zamora

"Instructions for My Funeral," "Dancing in Buses," and "'Ponele Queso Bicho' Means 'Put Cheese on It, Kid'" previously appeared in *Unaccompanied.*

Index

Contributor Biographies

Elizabeth Acevedo is a *New York Times* best-selling author. She is the winner of a National Book Award, the Carnegie Medal, the Michael L. Printz Award, and the *Los Angeles Times* Book Award, amongst other accolades. Her books include, *Beastgirl & Other Origin Myths*, *The Poet X*, *With the Fire on High*, and *Clap When You Land*.

Angélica Maria Aguilera is a Chicana writer from the San Fernando Valley in Los Angeles. Aguilera comes from a mixed family of Mexican immigrants and believes in poetry as a tool to decolonize narratives and unwrite shame. She is a Tedx Speaker and a finalist of the National Poetry Slam 2017, as well as the Women of the World Poetry Slam 2018.

Amanda Alcántara is a writer, journalist, and the author of *Chula*. Her work has appeared in the anthology *Latinas: Struggles & Protests in 21st Century USA*, and several media publications including NPR's Latino USA, *Remezcla*, the *Huffington Post*, the *Lily*, and the *San Francisco Chronicle*. She's a cofounder of *La Galería Magazine*. In 2017, Alcántara obtained an MA from NYU. Her thesis focused on the experiences of women residing in the border of the Dominican Republic and Haiti.

Penelope Alegria has performed spoken word across the Chicagoland area as a member of Young Chicago Author's artistic apprenticeship. Her work was featured in, or is forthcoming in, *La Nueva Semana, Muse/A Journal*. Her poem, "To: that nought in da jcemestry," is a Brain Mill Press editor's pick. Penelope's work will be animated and showcased at international film festivals for ARTS by the People's "Moving Words" initiative.

Nico Alvarado's poetry and prose have appeared in *Buzzfeed, Boston Review, Harvard Review*, and *Western Humanities Review*. He lives with his family in Colorado.

Savuth Thor

Diannely Antigua is a Dominican American poet and educator, born and raised in Massachusetts. Her debut collection, *Ugly Music*, was the winner of the YesYes Books' Pamet River Prize. A graduate of the MFA program at NYU, she is the recipient of fellowships from CantoMundo, Community of Writers, and the Fine Arts Work Center summer program. Her heart is in Brooklyn.

Ani Schreiber

José Angel Araguz is a CantoMundo fellow and the author of seven chapbooks as well as the collections *Everything We Think We Hear*, *Small Fires*, and *Until We Are Level Again*. His poems, prose, and reviews have appeared in *Crab Creek Review*, *Prairie Schooner*, and the *Bind*. He runs the poetry blog *Friday Influence* and teaches at Suffolk University where he is also the editor in chief of *Salamander Magazine*.

Lory Bedikian

William Archila is author of *The Art of Exile*, 2010 International Latino Book Award, and *The Gravedigger's Archaeology*, 2013 Letras Latinas/Red Hen Poetry Prize. His work has been published in *American Poetry Review*, *AGNI*, *Georgia Review*, *Los Angeles Review of Books*, *Prairie Schooner*, *Tin House*, and the anthologies *Theatre Under My Skin: Contemporary Salvadoran Poetry* and *The Wandering Song: Central American Writing in the United States*.

Billy Bustamante

Ashley August is an Afro-Latina actress, author, playwright, activist, third-ranked woman poet in the world, ASTEP at Juilliard fellow, and NYC's 2013 youth poet laureate, and was recently named one of the *New York Times* "30 Under 30 Most Influential People." With Belize and Brooklyn embedded into her (he)art, August is motivated to speak the unsaid truth and push the boundaries of art to new realms.

Erica Sanchez-Vazquez

Naomi Ayala Santiago is the author of the books of poetry *Wild Animals on the Moon*, *This Side of Early*, and *Calling Home: Praise Songs and Incantations*. A freelance writer and editor, she teaches poetry and memoir to English-language learners at the Carlos Rosario School via the Write Who You Are Program, a partnership between the school and the Writer's Center in Bethesda, Maryland. Naomi is also the award-winning translator of the poetry collection *The Wind's Archeology*.

Crystal Stella Becerril

Crystal Stella Becerril is a writer, cultural critic, independent journalist, and community and labor organizer working at the intersection of Xicana Marxist Feminism, class struggle, and the politics of cultural production and exchange. She is the cofounder of SAL(T): Xicana Marxist Tho(ugh)ts and the poetry editor at *Red Wedge* magazine. She lives and works in Brooklyn but calls the South Side of Chicago home.

Maya Washington

Sara Borjas is a Xicanx pocha and a Fresno poet. Her debut collection of poetry, *Heart Like a Window, Mouth Like a Cliff* was published by Noemi Press in 2019. Sara is a 2017 CantoMundo fellow and the recipient of the 2014 Blue Mesa Poetry Prize. She lives in Los Angeles but stays rooted in Fresno. Find her @saraborhaz.

patri hadad

Daniel Borzutzky is a poet and translator. His latest books are *Lake Michigan*, a finalist for the 2018 Griffin International Poetry Prize, and *The Performance of Becoming Human*, winner of the 2016 National Book Award for Poetry. His translation of Galo Ghigliotto's *Valdivia* won the 2017 National Translation Award. He teaches in the English and Latin American and Latino Studies Departments at the University of Illinois at Chicago.

Tehan Ketema

Sarah Bruno is a Puerto Rican Chicago South Side Native, a PhD candidate in the Cultural Anthropology program at University of Wisconsin-Madison, and a recipient of First Wave Hip-Hop and Urban Arts full-tuition scholarship. Her work is published in the *Acentos Review*, and she has performed throughout the country, competed at CUPSI, and is a Louder Than A Bomb and Louder Than A Bomb University champion.

Brenda Hernandez

Melissa Castro Almandina is a Xicana poet and artist from the Southwest Side of Chicago. She's a resident artist at AMFM Gallery and an editor at Brown and Proud Press. Her work has appeared in *Hooligan Magazine*, *South Side Weekly*, and numerous zines.

Andrés Cerpa is the author of *Bicycle in a Ransacked City: An Elegy*, and *The Vault*. A recipient of fellowships from the MacDowell Colony and CantoMundo, his work has appeared or is forthcoming in *Ploughshares*, *Poem-a-Day*, the *Kenyon Review*, *The Rumpus*, *West Branch*, and elsewhere. He was raised in Staten Island, NY and spent many of his childhood summers living in Puerto Rico.

Lorna Dee Cervantes is the author of *Emplumada*, *From the Cables Of Genocide*, *Ciento*, *Drive*, and *Sueño*. Awarded NEA grants, Pushcart Prizes, a Lila Wallace, state arts and best book awards, Cervantes is founder of MANGO Publications (first to publish Sandra Cisneros), and has presented at the Library of Congress, Dodge Poetry Festival, Walker Art Center, and Nuyorican Poets Cafe. She writes in Seattle.

María Fernanda Chamorro's poems and translations appear in *Pa'lante a la luz*, the *Wide Shore*, *Kweli Journal*, and elsewhere. María Fernanda holds received fellowships from CantoMundo, Callaloo Writers Workshop, and VONA/Voices of Our Nation. She founded Candela Writers Workshop to support Black-Latinx poets through the preservation and the advancement of Black-Latinx literary work. Chamorro is a Black Ecuadorian American and Washington, DC native.

Felicia Rose Chavez is a native New Mexican with an MFA in creative nonfiction from the University of Iowa. An award-winning educator, Felicia is currently at work on *The Anti-Racist Writing Workshop: How to Decolonize the Creative Classroom*, forthcoming from Haymarket Books in fall 2020. Find her at feliciarosechavez.com.

Victoria Chávez Peralta is a queer, first-generation Xicanx poet from the Chicago suburbs. They are currently a preschool teacher on the West Side and studying at Columbia College Chicago for poetry with a minor in education. Peralta has been published in the *South Side Weekly*, *Columbia Poetry Review*, and only performs at spaces that celebrate and advocate for women of color.

Briana Chazaro

Alan Chazaro is a high school teacher at the Oakland School for the Arts. His first poetry collection, *This Is Not a Frank Ocean Cover Album*, was winner of the 2018 Black River Chapbook Competition. His full-length book, *Piñata Theory*, is the recipient of the 2018 Hudson Prize. He will be traveling around, living in, and writing from South America and Mexico for the next year, so hit him up on Twitter at @alan_chazaro.

Davon Clark

Davon Clark is a Philadelphia-raised writer and photographer based in Chicago. His art looks to fill in the gaps left behind in coverage of the worlds that he lives in and peripheral to. He uses investigative journalism practices to inform how he approaches his work and its uses. He likes flowers and the little things in life.

Emmanuel Abreu

Bailey Alejandro Cohen-Vera is the author of the chapbook *Self-Portraits as Yurico* (Glass Poetry Press, 2020). His work appears or is forthcoming in *Muzzle Magazine*, *Southern Indiana Review*, *Boulevard*, *Raleigh Review*, *Sugar House Review*, *Boiler Journal*, and *Longleaf Review*, among elsewhere. An Ecuadorian-American undergraduate student in his final year at NYU, Bailey is currently finishing a thesis-length project on manifestations of revolutionary thought.

Constanza Contreras Ruiz

Constanza Contreras Ruiz is a Chilean in Michigan pretending to pass as a grad student. When this role weighs too heavy on her body, she starts screaming words to pieces of papers in the hopes of purging the effects of loss and those things lost in translation. Although a native speaker of Spanish, she's found it strangely difficult to find words in her own language to name what wants to come out of her mouth. Only recently has she begun to share writing with the world.

Karla Cordero

Karla Cordero is a descendant of the Chichimeca people from Northern Mexico. She is a Macondo, VONA, and CantoMundo fellow and recipient of The Loft Spoken Word Immersion Fellowship. Her work has appeared in *Bettering American Poetry*, *[PANK]*, *Anomaly*, and *BOAAT*. She is editor of *Spit Journal* and the author of the full-length collection *How to Pull Apart the Earth*. Follow her work at @karlaflaka13.

Hakim "Rebel Poet" Coriano is a Nuyorican activist, musician, songwriter, producer, and performance poet who has performed at Langston Hughes House, Nuyorican Poets Cafe, New York Poetry Festival, and "Capicu" Cultural Showcase. Born in Caguas, Puerto Rico, and partly raised in Long Island, New York, Rebel Poet is an eternal student of life who is presently attending "The Academy of Art University" for music production and soundtrack design. His love for the arts spills onto the stage as he honors his ancestors.

Gabriel Cortez

Gabriel Cortez is a biracial poet, educator, and organizer of Panamanian descent. His work has appeared in the *New York Times*, NPR, and *Huffington Post*. He is a VONA fellow, NALAC grant recipient, and winner of the Judith Lee Stronach Baccalaureate Prize. Gabriel is a member of the artist collective, Ghostlines, and cofounder of the Root Slam, an award-winning poetry venue dedicated to inclusivity, justice, and artistic growth.

Caroline Karanja

Anaïs Deal-Marquez is a Mexicana poet based in the midwest who writes about home, food, magic, and ancestors. She has completed her first manuscript which is a testament to displacement, memory, and tradition that weaves her own migration story with those of the women in her family. Anaïs is committed to fostering spaces for immigrant and refugee writers to use their art as an anchor for dialogue and healing.

Danny Hastings

Caridad De La Luz is a writer and performer known as "La Bruja" whose work has been on radio, television, films, and both Broadway and off-Broadway stages. She raps, acts, sings, hosts, recites, dances, and performs stand-up comedy. She is one of America's leading spoken word poets and has been named one of the all-time "Top Twenty Puerto Rican Women Everyone Should Know." Visit CaridadDeLaLuz.com to learn more.

Florencia Alvarado

Carina del Valle Schorske is a writer and translator living between New York City and San Juan. Her essays and poetry have appeared in *Lit Hub*, *Longreads*, *New York Times Magazine*, *Bookforum*, *Gulf Coast*, and *small axe*, among many other venues. She is at work on her first book, a psychogeography of Puerto Rican culture, forthcoming from Riverhead Books.

Maria Esquinca

Jaquira Díaz is the author of *Ordinary Girls*, a summer/ fall 2019 Indies Introduce Selection, and fall 2019 Barnes & Noble Discover Great New Writers Selection. Her work has been published in *Rolling Stone*, *Guardian*, *Fader*, and *T: The New York Times Style Magazine*, and included in *The Best American Essays 2016*. She lives in Miami Beach with her partner, the writer Lars Horn.

Britton Renaissance

Jennifer Falú: MFA. Writer. International Slam Champion. Performer. Teaching artist. Panda. Mother. Assassin.

Eric Lee

Stefanie Clara Fernández is a Cuban American poet and journalist from Miami, Florida. Her work has appeared in NPR, *No Depression*, *Miami New Times*, and *Kalliope Literary* magazine, among others. She currently lives in Washington, DC, where she is a producer at the *Atlantic* and a contributor for NPR Music.

Shun Takino

Ariel Francisco is the author of *A Sinking Ship Is Still a Ship* and *All My Heroes Are Broke*. A poet and translator born in the Bronx to Dominican and Guatemalan parents and raised in Miami, his work has appeared or is forthcoming in the *Academy of American Poets*, *American Poetry Review*, *Florida Review*, *Guernica*, the *New Yorker*, and elsewhere.

Urayoán Noel

Malcolm Friend is a poet originally from the Rainier Beach neighborhood of Seattle, Washington. He received his BA from Vanderbilt University, and his MFA from the University of Pittsburgh. He is the author of the chapbook *mxd kd mixtape* and the full-length collection *Our Bruises Kept Singing Purple*, selected by Cynthia Arrieu-King as winner of the 2017 Hillary Gravendyk Prize.

Nicholas Nichols

Denice Frohman is a poet and performer from New York City. She's received fellowships and awards from CantoMundo, Leeway Foundation, National Association of Latino Arts & Cultures, and Blue Mountain Center, and is a Tin House Workshop alum. Her poems have appeared in *Nepantla: An Anthology for Queer Poets of Color*,

Women of Resistance: Poems for a New Feminism, Adroit Journal and elsewhere. She's featured on hundreds of stages from the White House to the Apollo, and co-organizes #PoetsforPuertoRico.

Ali Blumenthal

Alexis Aceves Garcia is a first-generation, genderqueer, Latinx and Indochinese poet from San Diego, California. In 2019, they were awarded a full fellowship as the teaching assistant for Catapult's inaugural twelve-month poetry generator workshop with Angel Nafis and were accepted into the Jack Jones Literary Arts Retreat as the Cisneros Poetry Fellow. They are currently working on their first book, *COMO MANGO* and living in Queens, New York.

Lynda Le

Benjamin Garcia works in HIV/HCV/STD and opioid overdose prevention in the Finger Lakes region of New York. He had the honor of being the 2017 Latinx Scholar at the Frost Place, 2018 CantoMundo Fellow at the Palm Beach Poetry Festival, and a 2019 Lambda Literary Fellow. His work has recently appeared or is forthcoming in: *Missouri Review, American Poetry Review, New England Review, Kenyon Review, Crazyhorse,* and *Best New Poets 2018.* Find him on Twitter at @bengarciapoet.

Ashley Johanna Garcia

Roberto Carlos Garcia is a poet, storyteller, and essayist who is rigorously interrogative of himself and the world around him. He writes extensively about the Afro-Latinx and Afro-diasporic experience and has been published widely. His second poetry collection, *black / Maybe: An Afro Lyric,* is available from Willow Books; his first collection, *Melancolía,* is available from Červená Barva Press. He is founder of Get Fresh Book Publishing and professor of English at Union County College.

R. Bruna

Suzi F. Garcia is the author of *Dear Dorothy: A Home Grown Fairytale.* An executive editor at Noemi Press, she is also a board member of the Latinx Caucus, a CantoMundo Fellow, and a Macondonista. Her writing has been featured or is forthcoming from the *Denver Quarterly, Ninth Letter, Fence Magazine,* and more. You can find her at suzifgarcia. com or on Twitter at @SuziG.

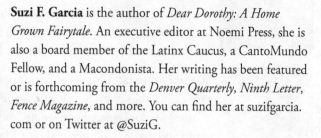

p. e. garcia

p. e. garcia is a features editor for *The Rumpus*. They are the author of *fictions&incantations*; *dear god, dear gordon*; and *p.e. garcia*. Currently, they are a PhD candidate in rhetoric at Temple University. You can find more of their work at avantgarcia.com.

Friends & Lovers Photography

Carlos Andrés Gómez is a Colombian American poet and author of *Hijito*, selected by Eduardo C. Corral as the winner of the 2018 Broken River Prize. Winner of the *Atlanta Review* International Poetry Prize and the Sandy Crimmins National Prize for Poetry, Gómez's writing has appeared in *New England Review*, *Beloit Poetry Journal*, *BuzzFeed Reader*, and elsewhere. For more, please visit: CarlosLive.com or connect via Twitter/Instagram at @CarlosAGLive.

Kezia Roberts

Mariana Goycoechea is a Guatemalan / Argentinian writer and educator based in New York City. Her work has been published in NYSAI Press, *The Rumpus*, the *Acentos Review*, *PALABRITAS*, *Fourth River*, and the *Selkie Lit* magazine. She is an alum of the Winter Tangerine Review and Tin House poetry workshops and has received funding from Sarah Lawrence. She holds fellowships from The Watering Hole, *Kenyon Review*, and the Juniper Institute. She has performed for the NYC Poetry Festival and the Capicu School of Poetic Arts.

Shauna J. Grant

Isa Guzman is a poet from Los Sures, Williamsburg, Brooklyn. They dedicate their work to exploring the traumas and hardships of the Boricua Diaspora. Their works appears in several publications such as *The Bridge* (Brooklyn Poets), the *Acentos Review*, *Rogue Agent*, and many more. They are pursuing their MFA at Brooklyn College and work with the Titere Poets collective exploring Latine masculinity on their podcast Pan Con Titeres.

Julian Sambrano

féi hernandez is a Mexican born, trans, nonbinary writer, visual artist, actor, and spiritual healer. They grew up undocumented in Inglewood, California. A Voices of Our Nations Art Foundation (VONA) fellow, féi's writing has been featured on NPR and in *Immigrant Review*,

Nonbinary: Memoirs of Gender and Identity, *Live Wire*, and *Hayden's Ferry Review*. Find their work at feihernandez.com

Tomás Riley

Leticia Hernández-Linares is a poet, interdisciplinary artist, and educator. She is the author of *Mucha Muchacha*, *Too Much Girl*, and coeditor of *The Wandering Song: Central American Writing in the United States*. Widely published, she has presented her poemsongs throughout the country and in El Salvador. A long-time community worker and Mission resident, she teaches in the College of Ethnic Studies at San Francisco State University. Visit joinleticia.com

Genesis Williams

Melinda Hernandez is an LTAB Indy and Team finalist from Chicago to the Bay Area at Stanford University, a 2x CUPSI finalist, and is featured on *Button Poetry*. Naturally, her love for poetry and music birthed a lyricist. In her short time as an emcee, Linda Sol has opened for well-known artists such as 2 Chainz, Ella Mai, and A.Chal. Her art is inspired by her family's resilience and self preservation.

Armando Ortega

Grecia Huesca Dominguez is a poet from Veracruz, Mexico. Her work has been featured in *Acentos Review*, and her debut children's book, *Dear Abuelo*, is available from Reycraft Books. She lives in Rockland County with her seven-year-old daughter.

Davidson Jeffers

Karl Michael Iglesias is a poet, actor, and director originally from Milwaukee, Wisconsin, now residing in Brooklyn, New York. His work can be read on *Apogee*, *Acentos Review*, *Breakwater Review*, *Florida Review*, *RHINO*, and *Kweli Journal*. He also explores verse driven theater as a facilitator at the BARS Workshop at The Public Theater and is a proud Poet Mentor in Residence at Urban Word NYC, where he teaches poetry and verse in New York City classrooms throughout the school year.

JP Infante (@infantejp) is a writer and teacher in New York City. He leads writing workshops and hosts the Creatives at Play Book Club. He holds an MFA in fiction from the New School and is a contributing editor for DominicanWriters.com. His writing can be found in the *Poetry Project*, *Manhattan Times*, and elsewhere. His short story, "Without a Big One," published in *Kweli*, won the

Benjamín Naka-Hasebe Kingsley belongs to the Onondaga Nation of Indigenous Americans in New York, and his abuelo immigrated from Havana's fourth floor. His first, second, and third books debut 2018, 2019, and 2020: *Not Your Mama's Melting Pot*, *Colonize Me*, and *Dēmos*. Peep his recent work in *Boston Review*, *FIELD*, *jubilat*, *Kenyon Review*, *New England Review*, *Oxford American*, and *Tin House*, among others. He is assistant professor of poetry and nonfiction in Old Dominion University's MFA program.

Esther Woo

Raina J. León is an Afro-Latina Philadelphian who believes in collective action and the liberatory practice of humanizing education. Her home communities include the Carolina African American Writers Collective, Cave Canem, CantoMundo, and Macondo. She is the author of three collections of poetry, *Canticle of Idols*, *Boogeyman Dawn*, and *sombra: (dis)locate* and the chapbooks *Areyto to Atabey: Essays on (the) mothering self in the Afro-Boricua* and, *profeta without refuge*. She is a founding editor of *Acentos Review* and a professor at Saint Mary's College of California.

Carlos Garcia

Sergio Lima is a first generation chilangringo. Raised in the Inland Empire of Southern California, he now calls Long Beach home. Mexico City, his father's hometown, calls to him always, saying, "Mijo, cuando regresas?" Sergio came to poetry first through hip-hop, then through teaching high school English in Lynwood, CA. His poems attempt to capture a life that resists containment; to search for where this struggle gives way to song.

Elizabeth Barahona

Antonio López received his BA in Global Cultural Studies and African and African-American Studies from Duke University. He has received scholarships to attend the Community of Writers at Squaw Valley, Tin House Summer Workshop, the Vermont Studio Center, and Bread Loaf. His work has appeared in *PEN/America*, *BOAAT*, *Palette Poetry*, *Huizache*, *Tin House*, and elsewhere. A proud Macondista, CantoMundista, and recipient of the 2019 Katherine Bakeless Nelson Award in Poetry from the Bread Loaf Writers' Conference, Antonio received his MFA (poetry) at Rutgers-Newark.

Tasneem Mandviwala

Adam Rubenstein

Hao Nguyen

Don Calva

Sheila Maldonado

J. Estanislao Lopez earned his MFA from the Warren Wilson Program for Writers. His work has appeared in the *New Yorker, Ploughshares, Harvard Review Online, the Shallow Ends*, and is forthcoming in the *Bedford Introduction to Literature*, 12th ed. He lives and teaches in Houston, TX.

Jessica Helen Lopez is emeritus City of Albuquerque Poet Laureate. A Chautauqua Scholar with the New Mexico Humanities Council, recipient of the Zia Book Award, and a Pushcart Prize Nominee, Lopez teaches for the Chicana and Chicano Studies Department at the University of New Mexico and at the Institute of American Indian Arts. Television host of the arts-based PBS show, *COLORES!*, Lopez is una madre, maestra, poeta y Chingona. She has traveled across international borders to perform and teach poetry. Lopez is the author of four collections of poetry and other anthologized works.

Kyle Carrero Lopez is a Black Cuban-American poet. Originally from North Jersey, he is the recipient of a TuCuba fellowship from CubaOne Foundation. He worked on leading their first Cuba trip focused entirely on Afro-Cuban culture. He is a poetry MFA candidate at NYU. His poems are published or forthcoming in *Poetry, Cincinnati Review, Florida Review, Grabbed,* and elsewhere. Find him at @kylelop3z.

Melissa Lozada-Oliva is the author of *Peluda* and is cohost of the podcast *Say More* with Olivia Gatwood. She performs her poems and teaches workshops across the country. Her works have appeared in *Cosmonauts Avenue, Redivider, Adroit Journal, Visible Poetry Project, Muzzle Magazine, Kenyon Review, REMEZCLA,* and BBC Mundo. She lives in Brooklyn.

Sheila Maldonado is the author of the poetry collection *one-bedroom solo*. Her second publication, *that's what you get*, is forthcoming from Brooklyn Arts Press. She is a CantoMundo Fellow and a Creative Capital awardee as part of desveladas, a visual writing collective.

David Tomas Martinez's debut collection of poetry, *Hustle*, was released in 2014 by Sarabande Books. Martinez is a Pushcart Prize winner, CantoMundo fellow, a Bread Loaf Stanley P. Young Fellow, and an NEA fellow. *Post Traumatic Hood Disorder*, a second collection, was released by Sarabande Books in 2018. Martinez lives in Brooklyn.

Jennifer Maritza McCauley is the author of *SCAR ON/ SCAR OFF*. She has received fellowships from the National Endowment for the Arts, Kimbilio, CantoMundo, and Sundress Academy of the Arts, and awards from Best of the Net, Independent Publisher Book Awards, the Academy of American Poets, and a special mention in the 2019 Pushcart Prize anthology. She currently lives and writes in Columbia, Missouri.

Aline Mello is an editor and writer. She's from Brazil and lives in Atlanta. She is an Undocupoet fellow and her work has been published or is upcoming in *New Republic*, *Atlanta Review*, *Grist*, and elsewhere.

Jasminne Mendez is a poet, playwright, educator, and award-winning author. Mendez has had poetry and essays published by or forthcoming in *Acentos Review*, *New England Review*, *Kenyon Review*, *Gulf Coast*, *The Rumpus*, and others. She is the author of two poetry/prose collections *Island of Dreams* and *Night-Blooming Jasmin(n)e: Personal Essays and Poetry*.

Lupe Mendez is a Texas Gulf Coast writer/educator/ activist and has been awarded fellowships to CantoMundo, Macondo, and the Emerging Poets Incubator. He cofounded the Librotraficante Caravan and is the founder of Tintero Projects, which works with emerging Latinx writers and other writers of color. He is the author of *Why I Am Like Tequila* and cohosts the literary podcast *Ink Well*. Mendez received his MFA from the University of Texas at El Paso and works in Houston.

James O'Connell

Jonathan Mendoza is a Boston-bred, Chicago-based Jewish and Mexican-American activist, spoken word poet, social justice educator, and musician. He is a National Poetry Slam Champion, winner of the 2018 Sonia Sanchez–Langston Hughes Poetry Prize, and a community organizer for housing, migrant justice, and youth power with Pilsen Alliance in Chicago's lower west side. Find books and updates through MendozaPoetry.com and at @jmendoza010 (Twitter/Instagram).

Ricardo Muñiz

Nancy Mercado is the 2017 recipient of the American Book Award for Lifetime Achievement, and was recently named one of 200 living individuals who best embody the work and spirit of Frederick Douglass by the Frederick Douglass Family Initiatives and the Antiracist Research and Policy Center at American University. She is the editor of the Nuyorican Women's Anthology published in *Voices E-Magazine*, Hunter College-CUNY. Visit her at nancy-mercado.com.

Samuel Miranda is a teacher, poet, and visual artist. Originally from the Bronx he has made his home in Washington, DC. He is the author of two collections of poety, *We Is* and *Departure*. His artwork has been exhibited in DC, New York, Madrid, and Puerto Rico. He collaborates with musicans, visual artists, and other poets, and curates a reading series at the *American Poetry Museum*.

Yesenia Montilla is an Afro Latina poet and translator, daughter of immigrants, and native New Yorker. Her poetry has appeared in *Prairie Schooner*, *Gulf Coast*, *Academy of American Poets Poem-a-Day*, and others. She received her MFA from Drew University in poetry and poetry in translation and is a CantoMundo Fellow. *The Pink Box*, her first collection, was long-listed for the PEN Open Book Award 2016.

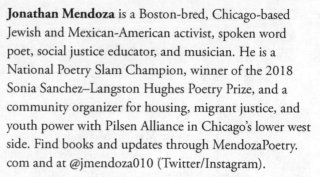

Anthony Morales is a Bronx-born, Nuyorican poet/educator/father who currently resides in Maryland. His work has appeared in *Aster(i)x*, *Hostos Review*, *Great Weather for Media*, *HBO's Def Poetry*, and *MANTECA! An Anthology of Afro Latin@ Poets*. He has self-published all of his collections, including *Vacio*, *A Good One Must Go*, and *Wandering Edge*.

Sherwin Bitsui

Juan J. Morales is the son of an Ecuadorian mother and Puerto Rican father. He is the author of three poetry collections, including the *Handyman's Guide to End Times*. He is also a CantoMundo Fellow, a Macondista, the Editor/Publisher of Pilgrimage, and the Department Chair of English and World Languages at Colorado State University-Pueblo. On Twitter at @ChairmanJuan.

Beth Jessee

Nadia Mota is a Chicana writer from southeast Michigan. She is currently an MFA candidate at the University of Michigan's Helen Zell Writers' Program. Nadia is the recipient of a Roy W. Cowden Memorial Fellowship and an Academy of American Poets Prize.

Marcus Jackson

John Murillo is the author of the poetry collections *Up Jump the Boogie* and *Kontemporary Amerikan Poetry*. He is an assistant professor of English at Wesleyan University and also teaches in the low-residency MFA program at Sierra Nevada College.

Rusty Wirek

Urayoán Noel is Bronx-based, Río Piedras-raised, and a professor at NYU. His latest books are *In Visible Movement: Nuyorican Poetry from the Sixties to Slam*, *Buzzing Hemisphere / Rumor Hemisférico*, and *Architecture of Dispersed Life: Selected Poetry by Pablo de Rokha*, which was longlisted for the Best Translated Book Award. Noel's poem "San Juan Starry Night" (2000) is part of the Museo de Arte de Puerto Rico's permanent exhibition.

Christine Castro

Mauricio Novoa is from Glenmont, Maryland, the son of Salvadoran refugees. He received his MFA from Queens University of Charlotte and has had his work published in *Blue Mesa Review*, *Acentos Review*, *La Horchata Zine*, *Latino Book Review*, and the anthology *The Wandering Song: Central American Writing in the United States*.

Marcos Vasquez

José Olivarez is the son of Mexican immigrants. His book of poems, *Citizen Illegal*, winner of the 2018 Chicago Review of Books Poetry Prize, was named a top book of 2018 by NPR. He holds fellowships from CantoMundo, Poets House, the Bronx Council on the Arts, and the Conversation Literary Festival. His work has been featured in the *New York Times*, *Paris Review*, and elsewhere. In 2018, he was awarded the Author and Artist in Justice Award from the Phillips Brooks House Association and named a Debut Poet of 2018 by *Poets & Writers*. In 2019, he was âwarded a Ruth Lilly and Dorothy Sargent Rosenberg Poetry Fellowship from the Poetry Foundation.

Sammy Ortega is a nineteen-year-old, queer-identifying male. They are the son of a Mexican migrant family. Their work emphasizes the queer and Chicano lenses within the Latinx community. Their poems push the narrative of a boy who unapologetically loves his femininity and the women in his life. They have poems published through the *Chicago Tribune* and Northwestern University Press. Sammy is always falling in love.

Gesi Schiling

Yaddyra Peralta is a poet and writer whose work has appeared in *SWWIM*, *Miami Rail*, *Ploughshares*, *Eight Miami Poets* anthology, and *Miami Herald*. She has taught writing at Miami Dade College, for Exchange for Change's writing in the prisons program, and for O, Miami's Sunroom. Yaddyra holds an MFA in creative writing from Florida International University. Yaddyra is now associate editor at Mango Publishing.

Jon Crispin

Willie Perdomo is the author of *The Crazy Bunch*, *The Essential Hits of Shorty Bon Bon*, a finalist for the National Book Critics Circle Award, *Smoking Lovely*, winner of the PEN Open Book Award, and *Where a Nickel Costs a Dime*, a finalist for the Poetry Society of America Norma Farber First Book Award. His work has appeared in *New York Times Magazine*, *Poetry*, *The Common*, and *African Voices*. He teaches at Phillips Exeter Academy.

Javier Perez is a Salvadoran-American poet. He is currently a PhD candidate in sociology at the University of Cape Town and got his BA in political science at Swarthmore College. Javier's poetry has been published in *Puerto del Sol, Up the Staircase Quarterly, Acentos Review, Label Me Latino/a,* and more. He is also recipient of the Thomas J. Watson Fellowship and Mellon-Mays Undergraduate Fellowship.

Abdiel Lopez

Janel Pineda is a Los Angeles-born Salvadoran poet, literary scholar, and activist whose family fled the US-sponsored Salvadoran Civil War. She is a Macondista and a founding editor and translator for *La Piscucha Magazine.* Janel holds a BA in English from Dickinson College and is currently pursuing an MA in creative writing and education at Goldsmiths, University of London as a Marshall Scholar. You can find more of her work at janelpineda.com.

Mario José Pagán Moralés, also known as Ponce, is a LaSopa alumni and founding member of the Títere Poets: a writing collective that addresses the intersection of poetry and the boundaries of masculinity, vulnerability, trauma, mental health and the Puerto Rican identity. He is a Pushcart Prize Nominee, and his work has been published in *Sofrito for your Soul, Acentos Review,* and Great weather for media's anthology, *Birds Fall Silent In The Mechanical Sea.*

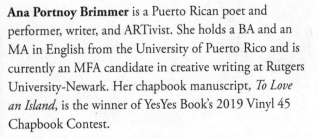

Ana Portnoy Brimmer is a Puerto Rican poet and performer, writer, and ARTivist. She holds a BA and an MA in English from the University of Puerto Rico and is currently an MFA candidate in creative writing at Rutgers University-Newark. Her chapbook manuscript, *To Love an Island,* is the winner of YesYes Book's 2019 Vinyl 45 Chapbook Contest.

Chris Setter

Noel Quiñones is a Puerto Rican writer, community organizer, and performer born and raised in the Bronx. He has received fellowships from CantoMundo, Sundress Academy for the Arts, the Poetry Foundation, and Poets House. His work is published in the *Latin American Review, Rattle,* and *Kweli Journal.* He is the founder of Project X, a Bronx-based arts organization, and is co-organizer of #PoetsforPuertoRico. Follow him at noelpquinones.com.

Brian Briganti

Gabriel Ramirez is a queer, Afro-Latinx poet. Gabriel has received fellowships from Palm Beach Poetry Festival, Watering Hole, Conversation Literary Arts Festival, CantoMundo, and Callaloo. You can find his work in publications like *Winter Tangerine, The Volta, Drunk in a Midnight Choir, VINYL,* as well as *Bettering American Poetry Anthology* (Bettering Books, 2017), and in *What Saves Us: Poems of Empathy and Outrage in the Age of Trump.*

Héctor Ramírez

Héctor Ramírez is a Xicano writer and educator and a child of immigrants. He is from Covina, California, currently lives in Colorado, and he is dedicated to activating his many privileges to confront oppressive systems and help people. His work has appeared in *Apogee, Muzzle Magazine, LIT, GASHER,* and elsewhere.

Anna Ramirez

Jacob Ramírez is a Mexican American poet and teacher from Merced, California. He holds an English degree from California State University, Fullerton and an MA in creative writing from Lancaster University in England. He has taught literature in China, the UAE, and Turkey. At present, he lives in Sonoma County with his wife and two children.

Tasha Gorel

Reyes Ramirez is a Houstonian. Reyes won the 2019 YES Contemporary Art Writer's Grant, 2017 Blue Mesa Review Nonfiction Contest, 2014 riverSedge Poetry Prize, and has work in: *Cosmonauts Avenue, Queen Mob's Teahouse, Deep Red Press, Latinx Archive, december magazine, TRACK//FOUR, Houston Noir, Gulf Coast, Acentos Review,* etc. He's received grants from the Houston Arts Alliance and the Warhol Foundation's Idea Fund. Read more of his work at reyesvramirez.com

Nicholas Nichols

Julian Randall is a living queer Black poet from Chicago. A fellow of Cave Canem, Callaloo, CantoMundo, and The Watering Hole, he is the recipient of a 2019 Pushcart Prize. He holds an MFA in poetry from Ole Miss. He is the author of *Refuse,* winner of the 2017 Cave Canem Poetry Prize and a finalist for an NAACP Image Award. He tweets mostly about poems at @JulianThePoet.

José Enrique Rico was born and raised in Bryan, Texas. He taught middle schoolers for two years before taking a brief hiatus from education. He wants to give a shout-out to all of his future students reading this bio (yo!). This is his first publication.

Pedro Rico

Monica Rico is a second-generation Mexican American who grew up in Saginaw, Michigan. She is an MFA candidate at the University of Michigan's Helen Zell Writers' Program and works for the Bear River Writers' Conference. Her poems have recently appeared in *BOAAT*, *Fifth Wednesday*, *Barrelhouse*'s *HEARD: A Tribute to Anthony Bourdain*, and Split this Rock's Poem of the Week. She is a 2019 CantoMundo Fellow and Macondista.

Amy Haberland

Joseph Rios is the author of *Shadowboxing: Poems and Impersonations*, winner of the American Book Award. He was named one of the notable Debut Poets by *Poets & Writers*. He is from Fresno's San Joaquin Valley. He's been a gardener, a janitor, a packing house supervisor, and a handyman. He is a VONA alumnus, CantoMundo fellow, and a Macondo fellow. He is a graduate of Fresno City College and UC Berkeley. He lives in Los Angeles.

Eliade's Photography

Sara Daniele Rivera is a Cuban/Peruvian artist, writer, translator, and educator from New Mexico. Her writing has appeared in *Origins Journal*, *DIALOGIST*, *Green Mountains Review*, and elsewhere, and in *Easy Street Mag* and the *Latinx Archive*. She was awarded a St. Botolph's Emerging Artist Award and the 2018 Stephen Dunn Prize in Poetry. Her community-based public art practice focuses on text-in-space as social intervention.

A. Roberts

stephanie roberts is a Québec-based, Black Latinx author of the poetry collection *rushes from the river disappointment*. Born in Panama, she lived in Brooklyn, New York, as an undocumented child before becoming a citizen. She has admired Cardi B since before that artist became famous famous.

Peggy Robles-Alvarado is a Lukumi and Palo priestess with MAEd degrees in elementary, bilingual education and an MFA in performance studies. She's a Pushcart Prize nominee, BRIO award winner, CantoMundo Fellow, and an International Latino Book Award winner. She's authored *Conversations with My Skin*, *Homage to the Warrior Women*, *The Abuela Stories Project*, and *Mujeres, the Magic, the Movement and the Muse*. Find her at @Robleswrites.com.

Anacaona Rocio Milagro is a native New Yorker and poet living in Washington Heights. She is the mother of Nirvana Sky and Zion Dario. Her father is from the Dominican Republic and her mother is from St. Thomas, the Virgin Islands. She is daughter of Oshun but adopted by Yemaya. She earned an MFA in poetry at NYU's low-residency program in Paris and an MPH at Columbia University. She earned a BA in social anthropology and journalism/creative writing with a minor in art from Baruch College. However, nothing compares to her education from the prestigious school of hard knocks.

Natalia Rodríguez Nuñez is a programmer and writer born in Mexico, raised in the border of Texas, and who now lives in Brooklyn, NY. Natalia's written and computational work explores the intersection of narrative, language, data, and code.

Wren Romero is a poet and performer from Phoenix, Arizona, living and working in Boston, Massachusetts where they study theater and make poetry with the Feminine Empowerment Movement Slam. They are a descendant of Tiguas, Gringos, and Mexican revolutionaries. Their forthcoming chapbook of poems was edited and published by Jamie Berrout for the Radical Trans Poetry Series. Follow them at @CUIDADX on Instagram and Twitter.

Jani Rose is a Puerto Rican poet, educator, and activist born in Spanish Harlem and raised in the Bronx. She is a Fellow of the Acentos Poetry Workshops, Pink Door, and VONA programs, uplifting writers of color. As cofounder of La Sopa, the School of Poetic Arts, she leads a workshop series in residence at the Nuyorican Poets Café. She released a chapbook, *Musings and Scribbles of a Nuyorican Geisha*, in 2016.

Noah Friedman

Raquel Salas Rivera es la Poeta Laureada de la ciudad de Filadelfia del 2018–19. Fue la recipiente inaugural del Premio Ambroggio y la Beca de Laureada, ambos de la Academia de Poetas Americanos. En el 2018, su cuarto libro, *lo terciario/the tertiary*, fue semi-finalista para el Premio Nacional del Libro y ganó el Premio Literario Lambda. Raquel vive por Puerto Rico, Filadelfia y un mundo libre de la supremacía blanca.

Raquel Salas Rivera is the 2018–19 Poet Laureate of Philadelphia. They are the inaugural recipient of the Ambroggio Prize and the Laureate Fellowship, both from the Academy of American Poets. Their fourth book, *lo terciario / the tertiary*, was on the 2018 National Book Award Longlist and won the 2018 Lambda Literary Award for Transgender Poetry. Raquel loves and lives for Puerto Rico, Philadelphia, and a world free of white supremacy.

Paola Graciela Salcido

Joel Salcido was born in the San Fernando Valley and raised in West Phoenix. He is the son of Mexican immigrants, a first-generation college graduate, husband, and father of three sons. Joel is a graduate of the MFA program at Arizona State University.

MJ Santiago

MJ Santiago is a queer Mexican American from Central Florida whose poetry has appeared in *Tinderbox Poetry*, *Scalawag*, and *The Shallow Ends*, among other places. Their first chapbook, *Baby Knife*, was published by Tenderness Lit in 2018. In addition to writing, MJ likes to take photos, pet their cats, and organize against systemic violence with their community of LGBT, queer, and gender-nonconforming people of color in Brooklyn.

Rachel Eliza Griffiths

Nicole Sealey, born in St. Thomas, U.S.V.I. and raised in Apopka, Florida, is the author of *Ordinary Beast*, finalist for the PEN Open Book and Hurston/Wright Legacy Awards, and *The Animal After Whom Other Animals Are Named*, winner of the Drinking Gourd Chapbook Poetry Prize. Formerly the executive director at Cave Canem Foundation, she is a 2019–2020 Hodder Fellow at Princeton University.

LaQuann Dawson

Sofía Snow is a Boston-raised multimedia artist, educator, and organizer. Her work has been featured in a range of publications, television, and theater, including *Boston Globe, Cosmopolitan, American Girl,* WWE Network, the Public Theater, and elsewhere. Sofía is currently the Director of the Office of Multicultural Arts Initiatives, home to the cutting-edge *First Wave Program*—the world's first and only full-tuition scholarship program for hip-hop and urban arts—at the University of Wisconsin-Madison.

Kai Richards

Christopher Soto is a poet based in Los Angeles, California. He is the author of the chapbook *Sad Girl Poems* and the editor of *Nepantla: An Anthology Dedicated to Queer Poets of Color.*

Virgil Suárez was born in Havana, Cuba in 1962. At the age of twelve he arrived in the United States. He received an MFA from Louisiana State University in 1987. He is the author of many collections of poetry, most recently *90 Miles: Selected and New.* His work is published in magazines and journals internationally. When he is not writing, he is out riding his motorcycle up and down the blue highways of the Southeast, photographing disappearing urban and rural landscapes. His tenth volume of poetry, *The Painted Bunting's Last Molt,* is forthcoming.

Nicholas Nichols

Daniella Toosie-Watson is a poet, visual artist, and educator from New York. She has received fellowships and awards from the Callaloo Creative Writing Workshop, the InsideOut Detroit Literary Arts Project, and the University of Michigan Hopwood Program. Her poetry has appeared in *Callaloo* and *Virginia Quarterly Review* and is forthcoming in *SLICE* magazine. Daniella received her MFA from the University of Michigan Helen Zell Writers' Program.

Vincent Toro is a Boricua poet, playwright, performer, and educator. He is the author of two poetry collections: *STEREO.ISLAND.MOSAIC.* and TERTULIA. Vincent is a professor at Bronx Community College, director of Cooper Union's Saturday youth arts program, a Dodge Poet, and a contributing editor for *Kweli Literary Journal*.

Carlie Febo

Amanda Torres is a loud-laughing Chicanafuturist writer, educator, and strategic dreamer originally from Chicago. She has committed her life to growing the field of youth arts and social justice work in Chicago, Boston, and NYC, and she currently works as a writer and facilitator in New York City.

Chris Disla

Sydney Valerio is a creative nonfiction, mixed-genre writer and performer. She daylights as an educator. In 2016 she wrote and performed *Matters: A One-Woman Show*. Her poetry is in several anthologies including *Mujeres, The Magic, The Movement & The Muse Anthology of Women Writers*. A 2019 BRIO award-winning poet and 2020 VOLCANISTA, she is currently working on her first book as an MFA student at the City College of New York.

Gabriel C. Pérez

Jesús I. Valles is a queer Mexican immigrant, educator, storyteller, and performer based in Austin, Texas, originally from Cd. Juárez, Mexico. Jesús is a 2019 Lambda Literary fellow, a 2019 fellow of the Sewanee Writers Conference, a 2018 Undocupoet fellow, a 2018 Tin House Scholar, and a fellow of the 2018 Poetry Incubator. Their work has been published in *Shade Journal, Texas Review, New Republic, Acentos Review, Quarterly West*, and *Mississippi Review*.

Elisabet Velasquez is a Boricua writer from Bushwick, Brooklyn. Her work has been featured in *Muzzle Magazine, Winter Tangerine, Centro Voces, Latina Magazine, We Are Mitú, Tidal*, and more. She is a 2017 Poets House Fellow and the 2017 winner of Button Poetry Video Poetry Contest. She is a 2019 Latinx Fellowship recipient of the Frost Place. Her work is forthcoming in Martín Espada's anthology *What Saves Us: Poems of Empathy and Outrage in the Age of Trump*.

Rachel Bosch

Rich Villar is a poet, essayist, and educator originally from Paterson, New Jersey. He is the author of *Comprehending Forever*. His poetry and commentary have appeared on HBO, NPR, and in numerous journals and anthologies. Rich leads poetry workshops and arts integration classrooms in high schools, middle schools, and educative spaces throughout the Northeast; he served as faculty for the Frost Place Conference on Poetry and Teaching in 2016.

Kaitlyn Marie Mercy

Nico Wilkinson is a poet, printmaker, farmer, and organizer based in Colorado Springs. They are the 2017 champion of the Capturing Fire International Queer Poetry Slam. They have authored and coauthored multiple books of poetry, most notably *Inauguration* with Idris Goodwin. They are the cofounder of Prickly Pear Printing and the founder of The Quaill Club, a living community for queer artists working toward cooperative sustainability.

Brittany Cronin

Javier Zamora was born in El Salvador and migrated to the US when he was nine. He was a 2018–2019 Radcliffe Institute Fellow at Harvard and holds fellowships from CantoMundo, Colgate University, the Lannan Foundation, MacDowell, the National Endowment for the Arts, the Poetry Foundation, Stanford University, and Yaddo. *Unaccompanied*, is his first collection. More info at: javierzamora.net

Jess Ewald

Joaquín Zihuatanejo is a poet, writer, and teacher from Dallas, Texas. Joaquín holds an MFA in poetry from the Institute of American Indian Arts. His new book, *Arsonist*, won the Anhinga-Robert Dana Prize for Poetry. Joaquín has two passions in his life: his beautiful partner Aída and poetry, always in that order.

About Haymarket Books

Haymarket Books is a radical, independent, nonprofit book publisher based in Chicago. Our mission is to publish books that contribute to struggles for social and economic justice. We strive to make our books a vibrant and organic part of social movements and the education and development of a critical, engaged, international left.

We take inspiration and courage from our namesakes, the Haymarket martyrs, who gave their lives fighting for a better world. Their 1886 struggle for the eight-hour day—which gave us May Day, the international workers' holiday—reminds workers around the world that ordinary people can organize and struggle for their own liberation. These struggles continue today across the globe—struggles against oppression, exploitation, poverty, and war.

Since our founding in 2001, Haymarket Books has published more than five hundred titles. Radically independent, we seek to drive a wedge into the risk-averse world of corporate book publishing. Our authors include Noam Chomsky, Arundhati Roy, Rebecca Solnit, Angela Y. Davis, Howard Zinn, Amy Goodman, Wallace Shawn, Mike Davis, Winona LaDuke, Ilan Pappé, Richard Wolff, Dave Zirin, Keeanga-Yamahtta Taylor, Nick Turse, Dahr Jamail, David Barsamian, Elizabeth Laird, Amira Hass, Mark Steel, Avi Lewis, Naomi Klein, and Neil Davidson. We are also the trade publishers of the acclaimed Historical Materialism Book Series and of Dispatch Books.

Also Available from Haymarket Books

Aftershocks of Disaster: Puerto Rico Before and After the Storm
Edited by Yarimar Bonilla and Marisol LeBrón

The Battle For Paradise: Puerto Rico Takes on the Disaster Capitalists
Naomi Klein

No One Is Illegal: Fighting Racism and State Violence on the U.S.-Mexico Border
Justin Akers Chacón and Mike Davis

Radicals in the Barrio: Magonistas, Socialists, Wobblies, and Communists in the Mexican-American Working Class
Justin Akers Chacón

Solito, Solita: Crossing Borders with Youth Refugees from Central America
Edited by Jonathan Freedman and Steven Mayers

CPSIA information can be obtained
at www.ICGtesting.com
Printed in the USA
BVHW030757270420
578463BV00003B/6